GALL.

See p. 152.

AN

INTRODUCTION

TO

PHRENOLOGY.

BY

ROBERT MACNISH, LL. D.

Author of "The Anatomy of Drunkenness" and "The Philosophy of Sleep," and Member of
the Faculty of Physicians and Surgeons of Glasgow.

SECOND EDITION,

ENLARGED, AND ILLUSTRATED BY THIRTY FOUR ENGRAVINGS.

GLASGOW:
JOHN SYMINGTON & CO.
EDINBURGH:—OLIVER AND BOYD.
LONDON:—WHITTAKER & CO.

MDCCCXXXVII.

TO

ROBERT COX, Esq.

CONSERVATOR OF THE MUSEUM OF THE PHRENOLOGICAL SOCIETY,
EDINBURGH,

THIS WORK

IS INSCRIBED, BY HIS FRIEND,

THE AUTHOR.

PREFACE

TO

THE SECOND EDITION.

THE success of this work has greatly exceeded the expectations of the author. Two thousand copies of the first edition were issued, and six months sufficed to exhaust the whole number. The book has also been printed by Messrs. Marsh, Capen, and Lyon of Boston, in the United States, and with every prospect of an equally rapid circulation in that country. These circumstances speak well for Phrenology, both in Great Britain and America. In the present edition, the work wears an entirely new aspect. It has been, in a great measure, re-written; and besides much new matter, contains a series of illustrations in wood, executed by Mr. Bruce of Edinburgh, the most skilful engraver of phrenological subjects in this country. The method of question and answer, the propriety of which at first seemed doubtful, appears to have been generally approved of. For a short treatise on a debateable subject like Phrenology it is well adapted, in so far as it affords an opportunity of bringing prominently forward all the objections, however important or frivolous, which have been made to the science, and of meeting them with suitable replies.

R. M.

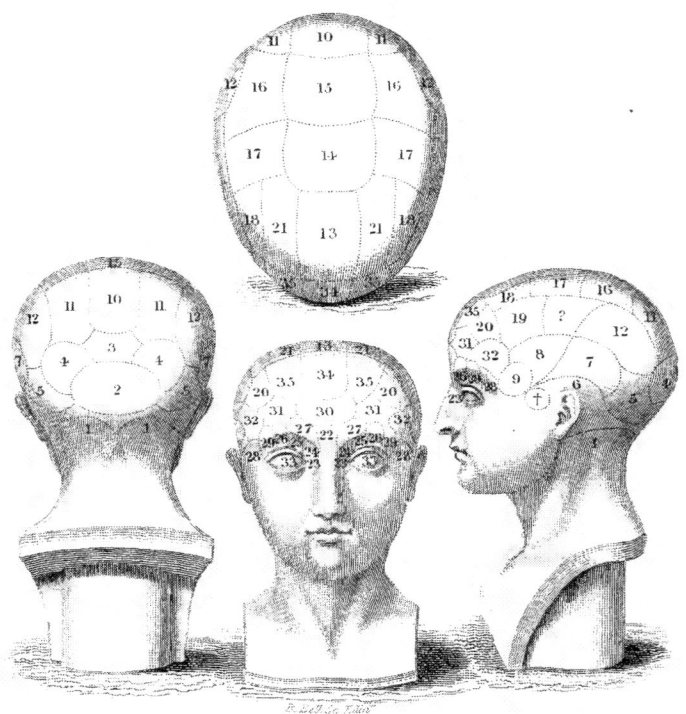

NAMES OF THE PHRENOLOGICAL ORGANS,

REFERRING TO THE FIGURES INDICATING THEIR RELATIVE POSITIONS.

AFFECTIVE		INTELLECTUAL	
I. PROPENSITIES.	*II. SENTIMENTS.*	*I. PERCEPTIVE.*	*II. REFLECTIVE.*
1 Amativeness	10 Self-esteem	22 Individuality	34 Comparison
2 Philoprogenitiveness	11 Love of Approbation	23 Form	35 Causality
3 Concentrativeness	12 Cautiousness	24 Size	
4 Adhesiveness	13 Benevolence	25 Weight	
5 Combativeness	14 Veneration	26 Colouring	
6 Destructiveness	15 Firmness	27 Locality	
7 Alimentiveness	16 Conscientiousness	28 Number	
7 Secretiveness	17 Hope	29 Order	
8 Acquisitiveness	18 Wonder	30 Eventuality	
9 Constructiveness	19 Ideality	31 Time	
	? Unascertained	32 Tune	
	20 Wit or Mirthfulness	33 Language	
	21 Imitation		

CLASSIFICATION OF THE FACULTIES.

ORDER I.—FEELINGS, OR AFFECTIVE FACULTIES.

Genus I.—Propensities.

1. Amativeness.
2. Philoprogenitiveness.
3. Concentrativeness.
4. Adhesiveness.
5. Combativeness.
6. Destructiveness.

† Alimentiveness.
   Love of Life.
7. Secretiveness.
8. Acquisitiveness.
9. Constructiveness.

Genus II.—Sentiments.

Species 1.—Inferior Sentiments.

10. Self-Esteem.
11. Love of Approbation.
12. Cautiousness.

Species 2.—Superior Sentiments.

13. Benevolence.
14. Veneration.
15. Firmness.
16. Conscientiousness.
17. Hope.
18. Wonder.
19. Ideality.
20. Wit.
21. Imitation.

ORDER II.—INTELLECTUAL FACULTIES.

GENUS I.—THE EXTERNAL SENSES.

Feeling.   Hearing.
Taste.   Sight.
Smell.   Mechanical Resistance.

GENUS II.—THE PERCEPTIVE, OR KNOWING FACULTIES.

Species 1.—Intellectual Faculties which take cognizance of the existence of external objects, and their physical qualities.

22. Individuality.   25. Weight.
23. Form.   26. Colouring.
24. Size.

Species 2.—Intellectual Faculties which take cognizance of the relations of external objects.

27. Locality.   31. Time.
28. Number.   32. Tune.
29. Order.   33. Language.
30. Eventuality.

GENUS III.—REFLECTIVE FACULTIES.

34. Comparison.   35. Causality.

INTRODUCTION.

My first ideas of Phrenology were obtained from Dr. Gall himself, its founder, whose lectures I attended in Paris during the year 1825. Before that time I, in common with almost all who are ignorant of the subject, spoke of it with great contempt, and took every opportunity of turning it into ridicule. The discourses of this great man, and several private conversations which I had the honour of holding with him, produced a total change in my ideas, and convinced me that the doctrines he taught, so far from deserving the absurd treatment which they then generally met with, were, in themselves, highly beautiful as expositions of the human mind in its various phases, and every way worthy of attention. Much reflection and many appeals to nature, since that period, have satisfied me of their truth.

Few subjects have encountered such persevering hostility as the doctrines in question; and persons now commencing the study can have little idea of the gross insults heaped upon its early cultivators by those who pretended to rule public opinion in matters of science and literature. Such usage, however, is not without many parallels in the history of the world. Persecution is the reward of innovation in whatever form that appears. To the truth of this assertion the banishment of Pythagoras, the poison cup of Socrates and the dungeon gloom of Galileo bear ample testimony. In our own country the sublime discoveries of Newton were long violently opposed, and Harvey, for ascertaining the most important fact in modern physiology, the circulation of the blood, was rewarded with abuse and the loss of his practice. In France things were no better—Descartes, one of the greatest geniuses that ever lived, having had the charge of atheism levelled against him for maintaining the doctrine of innate ideas. The stale trick of representing discoveries in science as hostile to religion, has, indeed, always been a favourite one with the enemies of knowledge, and even in these comparatively enlightened times is frequently had recourse to by the designing and the ignorant. Nothing is more common than to hear modern geology denounced as at variance with the word of God, and its cultivators held up as a conclave of infidels; nor has Phrenology escaped the same absurd charge, in the face of the notorious truth, that it is openly advocated by some of the most intelligent and pious of our clergy, and that the parent Phrenological Society was founded by the Rev. Dr. Welsh, Professor of Church History in the University of Edinburgh.[1]

Had the hostility to the Phrenological doctrines been confined to the weak-minded and illiterate, the circumstance would have excited no surprise, but at the first announcement of the science we find it assaulted on all sides by the learning

---

[1] "I think it right to declare that I have found the greatest benefit from the science as a minister of the Gospel. I have been led to study the evidences of Christianity anew, in connexion with Phrenology, and I feel my confidence in the truth of our holy religion increased by this new examination. I have examined the doctrines of our church also, one by one, in connexion with the truths of our new science, and have found the most wonderful harmony subsisting between them. And in dealing with my people in the ordinary duties of my calling, the practical benefit I have derived from Phrenology is inestimable."—*Rev. Dr. Welsh. See Phrenological Journal, vol. v. p.* 110.

"That the religious and moral objections against the phrenological theory are utterly futile, I have from the first been fully convinced."—*Whatley, Lord Archbishop of Dublin.*

and reputation of Europe. These attacks it has calmly and dispassionately met, and who that has surveyed the contest will have the hardihood to say that it has not triumphed? A more striking instance of the impossibility of stifling truth, has never been presented to the world, than in the victorious struggle of this science.

One of the most virulent attacks upon the new doctrines was made in the 49th number of the Edinburgh Review by the late Dr John Gordon, who not contented with unfairly misstating them, according to the usual practice of their opponents, demeaned himself by indulging in acrimonious personalities against the characters of Gall and Spurzheim. This attack, which in truth displayed nothing but gross ignorance and unbounded misrepresentation, was duly met and its various delinquencies exposed by the latter of these distinguished men. Lord Jeffrey in the 88th number of the same able work repeated the assault, only, however, to meet with a confutation equally conclusive from the pen of Mr. Combe. The attack was elegant, lively and satirical, and written in a not ungentlemanly spirit, but the accomplished writer lacked knowledge of the subject, and fell an easy victim before the well stored armoury of facts and reasonings, with which he was encountered by his acute antagonist.[2] An elaborate article by Dr. Roget,

---

[2] Some of the observations in the Edinburgh Review are amusing. Take the following as examples:—

"To enter on a particular refutation of them, (the opinions of Gall and Spurzheim) would be to insult the understandings of our readers."— "We look upon the whole doctrines taught by these two modern Peripatetics, anatomical, physiological, and physiognomical, as a piece of thorough quackery from beginning to end; and we are persuaded that every intelligent person, who takes the trouble to read a single chapter of the volumes before us, will view them precisely in the same light."—"They are a collection of mere absurdities, without truth, connexion or consistency, an incoherent rhapsody, which nothing could have induced any man to have presented to the public, under pretence of instructing them, but absolute

in the supplement to the Encyclopædia Britannica, was also replied to by Mr. Combe, and from this article having been withheld from the new edition of the work, we may conclude that neither the doctor nor his publishers were satisfied with the success of their experiment. From the extensive knowledge of Sir William Hamilton, much was expected in the way of opposition, but he fared no better than his predecessors. The same may be said of Drs. Stone, Barclay, Prichard, Bostock, and in truth, of all who have attacked the science. The whole body of crusaders against Phrenology are characterized by one curious feature. Each individual combatant imagines that he has annihilated the doctrines, and that they will never more be heard of; each employs the same arguments as if they had never been used before; each is in a state of perfect ignorance, with respect to the manner in which these arguments have already been disposed of; and finally, each invariably gives a false and distorted representation of the science. Few of those who have written against it, have done so in a generous, truth-loving mood. An unaccountable spirit of hatred has confused their perceptions, and rendered men whose talents ought to have made them formidable in the field of controversy, weak and inefficient as children. Hence, in every contest with their opponents, they have been defeated; nor

insanity, gross ignorance, or the most matchless assurance."—" Such is the trash, the despicable trumpery, which two men calling themselves scientific inquirers, have the impudence gravely to present to the physiologists of the nineteenth century as specimens of reasoning and induction."—*Dr. Gordon, in No.* xlix.

" Every one of course, has heard of Dr. Gall's craniology, and seen his plaster heads mapped out into territories of some thirty or forty independent faculties. Long before this time, we confess, we expected to have seen them turned into toys for children, and this folly consigned to that great limbo of vanity to which the dreams of alchemy, sympathetic medicine, and animal magnetism had passed before it."—*Lord Jeffrey in No.* lxxxviii.

INTRODUCTION.   13

has this taken place because the phrenologists possessed the advantages of superior talent and logical acumen, but simply because they entered the arena backed by truth. Without this indispensable ingredient, the greatest natural powers go for nothing in a question of facts, and with it the meanest become formidable.[3]

Great progress has been made by the science within the last ten years, especially in Great Britain, France, and the United States. It has met with considerable success in Sweden and Denmark, and has even succeeded in forcing its way into Italy. The late Professor Uccelli of Florence was a phrenologist. For this heinous offence he lost his chair in the university of that city, and was persecuted with all the blind malice of bigotry and intolerance. Two of the best phrenologists in the north, are Drs. Hoppe and Otto, both eminent Danish physicians, the latter Professor of Materia Medica, and Medical Jurisprudence in the university of Copenhagen. Berzelius of Stockholm, the most illustrious of living chemists, has become a convert to the science, and Andral, Broussais, Cloquet, Bouillaud, Sanson, Voisin, Falret, and Vimont, who are among the greatest medical characters in the French capital, have done the same.[4] The

[3] Those who intend writing against Phrenology, will save themselves the trouble of repeating stale and often confuted arguments, by perusing the different attacks made on the science, and the answers which have been made to them. A full list of these attacks and replies will be found in an article entitled "Phrenological Controversies," in the Phrenogical Journal, vol. x. p. 150.

[4] Many other able physicians are also members. Among a multitude of non-medical names I find the following, some of them men of considerable eminence.—Blondeau, Dean of the Faculty of Law, David, the celebrated sculptor, the Duke of Montobello (peer of France), Julien director of the "Revūe Encyclopédique", Poncelet, Professor of the Faculty of Law, Comte, Professor of Philosophy to the Athenæum, Royer, Chief Secretary to the Administration of the Garden of Plants, Les Cases and Ternaux, members of the Chamber of Deputies, &c. &c.

conversion of the last of these eminent men is curious, and forms a memorable fact in the history of Phrenology. Having attended Gall, he thought he could easily refute his doctrines, and for this purpose made a vast collection of specimens, chiefly of skulls of the lower animals; but the very evidence he was thus accumulating for the overthrow of the science had entirely the opposite effect. It satisfied him of its truth, and led to the publication of his magnificent work on " Human and Comparative Phrenology." A Phrenogical Society, numbering among its members many of the ablest scientific and literary men of Paris, has for some years been in active existence. By this body, a journal, exclusively devoted to the subject, and containing many admirable papers, is regularly published. Great zeal for Phrenology exists in the United States. Dr. Caldwell of Lexington, Kentucky, has written with uncommon talent upon the subject, and a valuable work entitled "Annals of Phrenology" is issued periodically at Boston. In that city a Phrenological Library is in the course of publication, consisting of reprints of all the best works which have appeared on the science, embodying also a translation, in six volumes, of Dr. Gall's unrivalled work *Sur les Fonctions du Cerveau.* Mr. Lawrence, one of the first surgeons and physiologists in this country, is favourable to the doctrines. In London, they have been supported with great power of reasoning by Dr. Elliotson; and such able physicians as Mackintosh of Edinburgh, Marsh of Dublin, and Barlow of Bath, have not hesitated openly and unscrupulously to adopt them. For more than ten years the Medico-Chirurgical Review and Lancet, the ablest medical periodicals in Great Britain, have honourably distinguished themselves in defence of the same cause. In Germany the science has prospered less than almost any where else in civilized Europe, thus verifying the old adage that "prophets are never esteemed in their own country." Even there, however, the rapid sale of a recent translation of Mr. Combe's "System of Phrenology," by Dr. Hirschfeld of Bremen, proves that public attention has at length been awakened to it; and there are good grounds for believing that the celebrated Blumenbach, contrary to the general understanding upon the subject, decidedly favours its pretensions.[5] Yet we are told that no men of eminence, have become converts to the science. The names here recorded sufficiently refute this assertion; and the Phrenological Societies of London, Edinburgh, and Paris, can boast of names inferior in talent and reputation to none in Europe. Considering the opposition which Gall's doctrines have met with, their acceptance by so large a portion of the public, is matter of wonder rather than otherwise. Newton's sublime discoveries met with no such prompt reception. They were long acrimoniously opposed in his own country, and at his death, more than forty years after the publication of the Principia, he had not above twenty followers on the Continent.[6]

The advance which Phrenology has made against the vast difficulties it has had to encounter, is indeed matter of congratulation, but much remains yet to be achieved. The weight of the Universities, and other seats of learning, bears strongly against it. There the metaphysics of the schools have been entrenched for ages, and will not surrender without a desperate struggle. The middle-aged and the elderly of the existing race, must die out before the new philosophy displays its full power. It is among the young, those whose minds have not been pre-occupied by other systems, and

[5] See Phrenological Journal, vol. viii. p. 531.

[6] For a complete account of the present state of the science, the reader is referred to Mr. Watson's excellent work, entitled "Statistics of Phrenology."

whose judgments are yet free and unshackled, that it is spreading most triumphantly. Its simple, intelligible and eminently practical character fits it admirably for unsophisticated youth, and it is pleasing to behold the steady progress which it is making among the young of both sexes. Even into colleges it is finding an entrance. Students in the metaphysical classes are beginning to imbue their essays with phrenological doctrines, either openly or in disguise, to the great horror of their professors, some of whom have thought fit to denounce, *ex căthedra*, the hundred-headed monster which has thus presumed to show its detested presence within the walls of Alma Mater.

Some people declare that they believe in the general principles of Phrenology, but not in its details. It would be far better to reject the science altogether, than indulge in such unmeaning perversion of language. All general principles are made up from details, and if the latter are faulty so must be the former. To say that we believe in the integrity of a whole, yet deny the soundness of the parts composing it is a pure absurdity. What would be thought of that man's intellect who acknowledged a certain ship of war to be perfectly sound and sea-worthy, and yet declared the timbers of which it was constructed to be rotten? To admit the principles of Phrenology, and yet deny the details which give these principles existence, is not less preposterous.

It has been objected to the science that certain erudite bodies have expressed their disbelief in it. When, however, it is known that these bodies know little or nothing of its true character, this objection will not, with any man of sense, weigh a single straw in the balance. Newton's discoveries were not proved to be false, because the University of Oxford resisted them for half a century. The opinions of all the learned associations in Europe, are valueless upon a subject of which they are ignorant. Nor is the objection, that the majority of medical men are hostile to Phrenology better founded. Let it not be forgotten, that the most eminent members of the profession long opposed the doctrine of the circulation of the blood, now universally admitted by physiologists. On a matter which he has never studied, the opinion of a medical man is no better than that of another person; and the general ignorance of the profession regarding Phrenology, is too well known to require demonstration. The existing race of medical students, however, are beginning to pay due attention to it; and, by and by, a knowledge of the subject will be so generally diffused among practitioners, that he who is deficient in this respect, will be considered to have neglected an important branch of his professional studies. The light which this science throws upon the physiology and pathology of the brain, and especially on the numerous class of mental diseases, is immense, and can only be appreciated by those who have turned their attention to it.

The superiority of the phrenological doctrines over every previous system of mental philosophy, consists in this—that their truth can be demonstrated with the same facility as any fact in nature, and that their bearings on the practical workings of life are equally susceptible of demonstration. Unlike scholastic metaphysics, they are not built in the clouds, but have a tangible base to rest upon. Unlike them, they are not mere barren speculations, but can be turned to good account. If we look to the old philosophy, we find its cultivators talking of perception, memory, judgment, and imagination, as constituting the primary mental powers, and using the machinery of attention, association, and habit, to solve every obstacle which stood in their way. If a man had great difficulty in nicely discriminating shades of colour, it was owing to an early want of attention! If he were fond of music or poetry, this resulted from association! If he were capable of great concentrated application, this had its origin in habit! In short, perception, memory, judgment, and imagination, are to the sound philosophy of the mind what the four elements of fire, air, earth, and water are to modern chemistry; while attention, association, and habit may be said to represent Phlogiston, that convenient agent by which every difficulty was at once got rid of. It is no proof of the soundness of this crude theory, that it was adopted by great names. In the dawn of every science, talents of the first order often got widely astray. Roger Bacon, Albertus Magnus, Raymond Lully, Van Helmont, and Paracelsus believed in the Elixir Vitae and the Philosopher's Stone; and, till a comparatively recent period, the Stahlian theory was in general acceptation among chemists. The same holds true with the philosophy of mind. Previous to Gall's great discovery, no proper method of investigating mental phenomena was known to metaphysicians, and gross errors and misconceptions consequently existed. We were gravely told, that the human mind was like a sheet of blank paper, on which any impression could be made; that all men were by nature precisely alike, and that variety of talent and disposition depended upon circumstances. The currency which such doctrines obtained, demonstrates a state of ignorance with respect to the mind, not inferior to that of physical science which existed in the days of the alchymists. Gall was the first person who laid the axe to the root of this barren tree, and planted a better in its place. If any man proceeded upon the strictest principles of the inductive philosophy, it was this illustrious individual. His inferences were sternly deduced from facts which came under his notice, and no one was ever less of a theorist. The method upon which he proceeded, has been rigidly followed by his disciples; and though none of them

INTRODUCTION. 19

have equalled their master in originality or grasp of mind, they may at least lay claim to the merit of being actuated by the same spirit of investigation, and of endeavouring, like him, to draw their knowledge directly from the book of nature. If they have failed, the fault is chargeable upon their own want of acuteness, and not upon the mode had recourse to by them, for the purpose of eliciting truth.

As people get acquainted with Phrenology, and the vast number of important points on which it bears, the opposition which it has hitherto encountered will gradually cease. This consummation is fast taking place, even already. Converts are daily flocking to its ranks, and those who still stand aloof are beginning to speak of it with some degree of respect. The hostile efforts of the press will, for a time, continue to check its onward march, but those are rapidly giving way before increasing knowledge. In the meantime, some of the public prints abound with ingenious inventions to its prejudice. Every paragraph is eagerly inserted if it only bear against Phrenology. We are daily told of blunders committed by *expert* Phrenologists, in their attempts to predicate character, from examination of the head.[7] If a notorious criminal is executed, we may calculate on being

---

[7] For example, the story of Dr. Spurzheim and the bust of Lord Pomfret, as exposed in the sixth volume of the Phrenological Journal; or the equally veracious one of Mr. Combe being imposed upon by a cast moulded from a Swedish turnip. There is no end to such impudent fictions. The alleged blunders of expert phrenologists are, in fact, mere weak inventions of the enemy, for the purpose of demolishing by fraud what they cannot encounter by fair argument. There have not even been awanting instances of individuals writing out characters, the very reverse of their own, and palming them off as phrenological failures. I know an instance of this kind, and another is related by Mr. Combe in his letter to Lord Jeffrey. Talking of the Swedish turnip, the facetious personage who made the unsuccessful attempt to play off this hoax against Phrenology, has since studied the science, and become a complete convert to its truth. See page 13 of that interesting volume, entitled " *Selections from the Phrenological Journal,*" recently published.

informed that he possessed a splendid development, and so forth! Lacenaire, the assassin of sixteen individuals, had, we were told, such a formation of head as Gall would have assigned to a mild, kind-hearted, religious character. Hare was formidable in the regions of Benevolence and Ideality, and Fieschi remarkably deficient in those of Firmness and Destructiveness! All such stories are idle inventions, without a particle of truth, but they serve the intended purpose of imposing upon the unwary, and exciting a hostile feeling towards Phrenology.

In whatever way we view this science, its tendency is excellent. It is eminently useful to the medical practitioner, by turning his attention forcibly to the state of the brain and whole nervous system, in health and disease—to those who have the charge of lunatics and criminals—to those concerned in the administration of justice [8] —to parents, in the intellectual, moral, and physical management of their children, and, in short, to every class of society. Grievous errors in education, in the treatment of malefactors, and in what are called mental diseases, are constantly committed,

[8] Were Phrenology known, as it ought to be, by judges and public prosecutors, we should not behold the revolting spectacle of lunatics perishing on the scaffold, as is too often the case in Great Britain; nor medical men giving it as their opinion, that the unfortunates who have so perished were responsible agents. There is something appalling in the thought of inflicting death on creatures whom God has stricken with idiocy or derangement, merely because those who try them, and those who testify to their fitness for being put upon trial, are ignorant of the nature of their malady. No man can now doubt, that Barclay who was hanged at Glasgow, and Howison who suffered the same fate at Edinburgh, were disordered in intellect to a degree which placed them beyond the pale of responsibility. The light thrown by Phrenology on Mental Derangement is most valuable, and will, in time, be so reflected upon Criminal Jurisprudence as to render such dreadful misapplication of the law a rare, or rather an impossible, occurrence. In the third and tenth volumes of the Phrenological Journal, there is some valuable information on the subject of Insanity and Crime. See also Dr. Combe's work on Mental Derangement, and the treatises on the same subject by Burrows, Conolly, and Esquirol.

from ignorance of the light thrown by Phrenology upon these important subjects. A science which is able to accomplish all this cannot be a trivial one; and time, the great arbiter, will yet render it ample justice, when every thing which has been said and written against it is utterly forgotten.

GENERAL PRINCIPLES.

What is the material organ of the mind?

The brain. The mind requires a material apparatus to work with; the brain is this apparatus. The brain itself, however, is not alleged by phrenologists to be the mind, any more than a musical instrument is music, the tongue taste, or the ears hearing. When the strings of a harp or violin are touched in a particular manner we have music. When the brain is in certain states we have displays of the mental faculties. Of the mind, as a separate entity, we can know nothing whatever, and we must judge of it in the only way in which it comes under our cognizance.[9]

What reason is there to infer that the mind is manifested through the medium of the brain?

We have undoubted evidence of this in the following and many similar facts. When a person receives a violent blow on the head—when blood or any other fluid presses upon the brain—or when a portion of the skull is beaten in—insensibility is a frequent, or rather a general occurrence.

---

[9] " The mind sees through the medium of the eye, just as it thinks or feels through the medium of the brain; and as changes in the condition of the eye deteriorate or destroy the power of vision, without any affection of the principle of mind, the obvious inference follows, that, in like manner, may changes in the condition of the brain destroy the power of feeling or of thinking, and yet the mind itself, or soul, remain essentially the same."—*Dr. Combe on Mental Derangement.*

A dose of opium, by acting on the brain, suspends the phenomena of mind; in like manner, when the brain is inflamed, the mental operations are disturbed. Did the mind act independently of the brain, no physical injury or irritation of the latter should have any effect upon the faculties; whereas, we find that the reverse is the case. Insanity, in fact, is nothing but cerebral disease inducing disordered mental manifestations. Finally, when the brain is extremely small, idiocy is the invariable result. Such a form of head, for instance, as is represented in the following sketch, is incompatible with the most ordinary degree of intelligence. The subject of the engraving was an idiot girl, aged fourteen, whom Dr. Spurzheim saw in Cork. The extreme deficiency of brain is very obvious.

Does the mind consist of one faculty or of several?
Undoubtedly of many. We have the passions of fear, love, attachment, pugnacity, &c.; the sentiments of benevolence, veneration, justice, &c.; besides a variety of other qualities, such as the powers of music, calculation, causation,

and many others. All these powers, susceptibilities, and emotions of the mind are called faculties ; each is distinct, and possessed by different individuals, in different degrees.

Since the mental faculties are so varied, how can a single viscus like the brain manifest them all ?

There is irresistible evidence to demonstrate that the brain is not a single organ, but in reality a congeries of organs, so intimately blended, however, as to appear one. Each of these is the seat of a particular mental faculty; so that, as the whole mind acts through the medium of the whole brain, so does each faculty of the mind act through the medium of a certain portion of the brain. Thus, there is a part appropriated to the faculty of Tune, another to that of Imitation, and so on through the whole series. The brain, in short, as Dr. Spurzheim observes, " is not a simple unit, but a collection of many peculiar instruments."

Upon what evidence do you found these assertions ?

The evidences are numerous. Were the brain a single organ, of which every part was employed in the manifestation of all the mental faculties, there could be no such thing as monomania, or madness on one point: if a portion of the brain were diseased, the whole mind should suffer; whereas, we often find that one faculty is insane, while all the others are perfectly sound. In like manner, fatigue of one organ should exhaust the whole, but we do not find this to be the case; for after overtasking the reflecting powers, we may be fully prepared to call others, such as Tune, Imitation, &c. into energetic activity. Dreaming, likewise, is inconsistent with the supposition that the brain is a single organ. If it were so, we should be either completely awake or completely asleep; whereas, in dreams, one or more faculties are in operation, while the rest continue in perfect repose. The perversion in madness, and the wakefulness in dreaming, of certain faculties, cannot otherwise be explained, than by supposing that each of these has a separate locality in the brain. It is only on the same principle that partial genius can be accounted for.

These are certainly strong proofs, but are there no others of a more direct and tangible description?

Many such. It is sufficient to mention that if, in a healthy brain, any particular portion is very much developed, the individual will be found to possess a more than usual energy in some particular faculty. Take, for instance, two heads, as nearly as possible alike in their general configuration, but differing strongly in shape at a certain part; the persons to whom they belong will be found to resemble each other in disposition, except in so far as the faculties connected with the organ or organs which lie at that part are concerned: here their characters will differ most materially.[10]

What is the science called which teaches all this?

It is denominated PHRENOLOGY, the merit of discovering which, and reducing it into a system, is due to the celebrated Dr. Gall of Vienna. Dr. Spurzheim, his disciple and associate, has also done much to extend and improve the science, which has been still farther advanced by the labours of Mr. Combe, and other ingenious men in this country and on the continent.

What were the circumstances which led Dr. Gall to the discovery?

They were partly accidental, and partly owing to the in-

[10] Sibbern, the celebrated professor of Logic in the University of Copenhagen, expresses himself as follows:—" If, upon the whole, the brain is such an organ for the mind, that the latter cannot act without the former, but is disturbed whenever the brain is morbidly affected, certainly nothing can be objected to the principle in Dr. Gall's doctrine, that certain faculties of the mind require certain modes of action in the brain, and have their appropriate organs in it. To assert that a talent for mathematics requires a special organ in the brain, is no more singular than to assert that thinking, in general, requires a well organized brain. Psychologically considered, Dr. Gall's doctrine is not at all improbable."

tuitive sagacity and excellent powers of observation possessed by that remarkable man. While a mere boy at school, he observed that such of his fellow-pupils as had prominent eyes were those with whom, in matters of scholarship, he had the greatest difficulty in competing. He might surpass them in original composition; but in exercises of verbal memory they left him far behind, and were invariably the best scholars. On leaving school and going to the university, he observed the same rule to hold good. The "ox-eyed" students, as they were called, always bore away the palm whenever the acquisition of languages was concerned. This fact struck him forcibly, but for a long time he knew not what to make of it. Some time afterwards, he had occasion to remark that one of his acquaintances, with whom he used to ramble in the woods, never lost his way, which Gall himself frequently did. This young man had two very marked prominences on his forehead, just above the root of the nose, while with Gall there were no such protuberances. On extending his observations, he found that persons so characterized acquired with great ease a knowledge of localities—that they found their way almost intuitively, as it were, in any route, however complex, if they had been there once before; and that those who wanted the marks in question had great difficulty in so doing. After reflecting deeply, he came to the conclusion that these differences of talent might depend upon the size of particular parts of the brain. This happy idea having once suggested itself, he followed it up with admirable skill and indefatigable perseverance, and at last ascertained distinctly, that the strength of the mental faculties is, *cæteris paribus*, in proportion to the size of those compartments of the brain by which they are manifested.

One man, then, with a certain organ larger than it is in another, will possess the faculty belonging to it in greater vigour?

Most certainly;—supposing the brains of both to be equally healthy, their temperaments the same, and the circumstances in which they have been placed, equally favourable for the excitement and cultivation of the particular faculty.[11] It is obviously as impossible for a person with a great deficiency of the organs of the moral sentiments, such as Benevolence and Conscientiousness, to be a virtuous character, as it is for the brain of an idiot to display the splendid intellect of a Milton or a Cuvier.

A large brain, therefore, other circumstances being equal, will be superior in power to a smaller one?

Facts place this beyond a doubt. A large-brained person acquires a natural ascendancy over another, whose cerebral system is smaller. A nation of small-brained people is easily conquered, and held in subjection; witness the facility with which the small-headed Hindoos were subjugated, and the extreme difficulty experienced in overcoming the Caribs, whose brains are large and active. The large size of the Scotch brain was probably one of the causes which rendered the permanent subjugation of Scotland by the English impossible. No man acquires a supremacy over masses of his fellow-men without a large head. The head of Pericles, who wielded at will the fierce democracy of Athens, was of

---

[11] The degree with which an organ will manifest its power, depends greatly upon the circumstances here mentioned. Temperament, in particular, has a powerful influence on the cerebral activity, and must be carefully borne in mind. There is another circumstance which modifies the vigour of an organ's manifestations, and that is the size of the organ in reference to others in the same head. If two men, for example, have the same absolute size of the organ of Tune, (the temperaments being similar) the natural strength of the faculty will be equal in each; but should Tune, in th one case, be the largest intellectual organ, then there will be a considerabl difference in the manifestation of musical power. The first person wi cultivate his organ of Tune almost exclusively, and thus greatly increas its energy: the other may cultivate it to some extent, but having othe faculties still stronger, he will exert them more, and thus the natural capa bilities of his Tune will never be brought fully out.

28   GENERAL PRINCIPLES.

extraordinary size. Mirabeau, whose thunders shook the National Assembly of France; Danton, who rode like an evil spirit on the whirlwind of the French Revolution; Franklin, who guided, by the calm power of his wisdom and virtue, the legislature of America, had all of them heads of uncommon size. That of Mirabeau is spoken of as enormous, and he is known to have possessed incredible force of character, as well as distinguished talent. Without great size of head, Mr. O'Connell never could have impressed himself so forcible as he has done upon the present age. There is not a single instance of any one with a small or moderate-sized brain wielding multitudes like the Irish "Agitator," or grappling triumphantly with the dangers of a troubled age, like the iron-hearted Cromwell, or raising himself from a private station to the most splendid throne in Europe, like the Emperor Napoleon. To accomplish such feats, not great intellect merely is demanded, but commanding force of character, arising from unusual size of brain.[12]

What is the average weight of the brain?

The brain, at birth, weighs, according to Meckel, about ten ounces. The usual weight of the male adult brain he estimates at three pounds five ounces and a half.[13] According to Virey

---

[12] Men in authority, such as military and naval commanders, governors of work-houses and prisons, managers of large establishments, magistrates and schoolmasters, should all have large heads; otherwise, let their moral qualities and talents be what they may, they will fail of insuring ready and spontaneous obedience. The power of mind derived from a large brain makes its possessor be feared and respected, while a small-brained person is felt to be feeble and ineffective. The wrath of the first is formidable, that of the other only excites laughter.

[13] Dr. Elliotson presented to the London Phrenological Society, the cast of the head of a male idiot, aged eighteen years, which measured only sixteen inches in circumference, and seven inches and three quarters from ear to ear, over the vertex. The cerebrum weighed but one pound seven and a half ounces, and the cerebellum but four ounces; in all one pound

that of the female is three or four ounces less. Farther observations, however, are necessary, to ascertain the average difference in this respect between the sexes, although the fact is undeniable, that, generally speaking, the female brain is the smaller of the two.

Does the female brain differ in any other particular from the male?

It does. Certain portions are larger and others smaller. Generally speaking, a woman's skull and brain, are longer in proportion to their breadth than those of a man. This point may readily be ascertained by taking even a cursory glance at the heads of the two sexes.

What follows when an organ is remarkably small?

Extreme feebleness of the faculty which is connected with it.

May not a large-brained person be an idiot?

Unquestionably; but in such a case the cerebral structure is in a morbid state. Generally speaking, however, when a full-sized brain gets diseased, there exists some active form of derangement, and not idiocy.

Will the exercise of an organ increase its size?

It is so maintained by some phrenologists, but a sufficiently large body of facts appears still wanting to set the matter completely at rest. If we work an organ vigorously, especially during youth, it is not unreasonable to suppose that its bulk may be thereby augmented; the analogy of the muscles favours such a conjecture. At all events, it is certain, that the energy and activity of the organ will be greatly increased. The lapse of ages of civilization, in any country, will, very probably, improve the form and quality of the national brain, by the continued action which this state

---

eleven ounces and a half. Compare this with the brain of Cuvier which weighed three pounds ten ounces four drachms and a half. Where the circumference of the adult head is under seventeen inches, mental imbecility is the inevitable consequence.

of society confers on the moral and intellectual organs, and the comparative inactivity in which it keeps the lower propensities.[14] The skulls of our ancestors, which have been dug up, give indication of an inferior moral and intellectual organization, and of stronger propensities than are presented by the average of heads at the present day.

May an organ be well developed, and yet incapable of manifesting its faculty in a powerful degree?

This may occasionally happen in consequence of a general or partial want of energy in the brain. It is most likely to occur in persons of a lymphatic temperament, where the cerebral circulation is carried on with little vigour. Sometimes a single organ becomes apathetic, while the rest are healthy. Isolated cases of this description form no objec-

---

[14] In the article "Hydrocéphale," in the twenty-second volume of the "Dictionnaire des Sciences Médicales," it is stated, that the heads of great thinkers frequently increase till fifty years of age. According to Itard, the head of Napoleon, which acquired an enormous development, was small in youth. The fact seems pretty well established, that if the brain is not exercised, it may actually diminish in bulk. In long protracted madness, it seems often to diminish, especially in the intellectual regions. Such was probably the case with Dean Swift, who, for some years before death, was in an imbecile state of mind. The portraits of that great man represent his forehead as much larger than it appears in his skull. Esquirol mentions the case of an insane female, whose forehead, on her admission into the hospital, was so large that he had a drawing made of it, but afterwards it became small and narrow. In the Phrenological Journal vol. iv. p. 495, the case of a deranged person is recorded, where the same event occurred. " His head increased in size during the progress of his insanity, and to such an extent that he observed the circumstance himself, and said that he required a smaller size in each successive hat that he purchased. His intellectual faculties were obviously feebler in the latter years of his life, for he became incapable of collecting money by presenting receipts, and performing some other little pieces of business which in former years he had accomplished, and his forehead very perceptibly diminished and retreated during the corresponding period. He accounted for the decrease in the size of the hats he required by ascribing it to the sublimation of his brain; he said he was becoming purely ethereal, and that the grosser particles of his head were evaporating daily."

ion to Phrenology, but rather prove its truth, in so far as they demonstrate that vigorous results cannot be expected from unhealthy organs.

Can the natural dispositions and talents of an individual be inferred by examination of his brain?

They can be predicated with great accuracy after such an examination; but it is necessary to take different circumstances into view, such as temperament, education, and example, as they modify, to a considerable extent, the character. A phrenologist, knowing these modifying causes, can speak with great precision after examining the brain.

Can actions be inferred?

No. These depend much on the circumstances in which the person is placed. A phrenologist, examining the head of Hare, would infer, that his mind was of a low and degraded order, that its tendency was towards cruelty and contention, and that his pleasures were all of a base kind; but he could not infer that he would necessarily commit murder. Hare became a murderer by the force of circumstances. He lived many years without committing murder; and when he did so, it was to obtain money to gratify his grovelling desires. Could he have readily procured money otherwise, it is not at all likely that he would have been guilty of the crime. Men always act from the strongest motives. The motives which induced Hare to murder, were unhappily, stronger than the restraining ones, and, therefore, he murdered.[15]

[15] Some people expect phrenologists to say, by an examination of the head, what actions a man will necessarily commit, but this is a childish piece of folly. The head of Hare was precisely the same the instant before committing his first murder as it was the instant after. All that a phrenologist could affirm on seeing such a head, would be that its owner had an organization, accompanied by dispositions which, in particular circumstances, would almost inevitably lead him to the commission of some atrocious crime. Hare was 36 when he commenced his horrible career. Supposing him to

Wherein consists the abuse of a faculty ?

A faculty is said to be abused when it acts in a degree too intense, or towards an improper object; also when it is active at an improper time, or in an improper place.

How are the faculties brought into communication with the external world ?

By means of the external senses. The organs of these senses (the ear, the eye, &c.) are connected with the brain through the medium of nerves, which convey the impressions made upon their respective organs to the cerebral mass, and thus give to the mental faculties a cognizance of what is occurring from without.

In predicating character, is it absolutely necessary to examine the uncovered brain?

No. Inferences may, in general, be drawn with great accuracy, during life, by examining the external surface of the head.

Does not the skull afford an obstacle to obtaining a correct idea of the shape of the brain?[16]

---

have died at the age of 35 he would not have had the stigma of murder attached to his name; but nevertheless he must have possessed the same tendency to commit crime as he manifested at a later period; and a phrenologist on being shown his head, and not knowing to whom it belonged, would infer accordingly, making allowance for the way in which such a character would be modified by circumstances.

16 The reader should make himself acquainted with the general anatomy of the skull, otherwise he will be at a loss to understand the references occasionally made to its particular parts. The bones of the skull-cap (that cavity which contains the brain) are as follows:—1. The frontal bone, which forms the upper and forepart of the head. 2. The occipital bone, which forms the lower and back part. 3. The two parietal bones, which lie between the frontal and occipital, and form the sides and top of the head. 4. The two temporal bones, which lie in the temples, and form the lower parts of the sides of the skull. 5. The ethmoid bone, which lies in the base of the skull, immediately over and behind the nose. 6. The sphenoid bone, which lies between the ethmoid and occipital bones, and supports the centre of the brain. These bones are united by seams, or sutures. The coronal

GENERAL PRINCIPLES.   33

This happens only in rare cases, and almost always at isolated points; the whole skull is seldom affected. In a vast majority of cases, the cranium gives a minutely accurate representation of the shape of the brain. In old age, however, the skull frequently becomes very thick, occasionally very thin, and at other times of very unequal thickness. In such cases, the form of the brain cannot be accurately ascertained during life.

Are the form and texture of the skull and brain influenced by insanity?

This is very frequently the case, especially if the malady has been of long continuance. The brain shrinks; its convolutions become narrower, and lose their turgescency. The skull, at the same time, becomes very thick, but instead of being soft and spongy, as in old age, it acquires great additional hardness and compactness of fibre, and has an appearance not unlike ivory. In two hundred and sixteen heads of maniacs, which were opened by Greding, a hundred and sixty-seven were very thick, without taking into consideration those, which, though of no unusual thickness, were remarkably hard. Of a hundred furious lunatics the skulls of seventy-eight were thick; and the same was the case with twenty-two out of thirty skulls of idiots. In such cases, therefore, the cranium does not in general, accurately represent the form of the brain, and here we are not to expect that just inferences of character can be drawn, any more than in very advanced life.

Is the skull formed before or after the brain?

The brain is formed first, and gives shape to the skull,

---

suture runs between the frontal and parietal bones, the lambdoidal suture between the parietal and the occipital, and the sagittal suture between the two parietals, along the centre of the head, stretching from the coronal to the lambdoidal suture. The temporal sutures join the temporal bones to the parietal, occipital, and frontal bones. The sphenoidal and ethmoidal sutures connect these two bones to each other, and to the rest.

which is moulded over it. The process of ossification does not commence till the seventh or eighth week of pregnancy, and is far from being completed at birth.

At what period does the brain attain its full size?

Great differences of opinion exist with regard to this point. According to phrenological writers, the brain does not attain its full size till between the twentieth and thirtieth year, while, according to Sir William Hamilton and the Wenzels, it arrives at its utmost magnitude at the age of seven. In such a conflict of totally different opinions, we must regard the point as undecided, although it seems incredible, that the brains of children of seven, are equal in size to those of full-grown men. I, for one, do not believe it.

After attaining its full size, does the brain ever diminish?

It does so in very old age, at which time the cranium, as already noticed, becomes frequently thicker, its inner layer retreating inwards, and either being followed by the outer layer, or leaving a considerable thickness of spongy diploe between them.

Is the substance of the brain of the same consistence at every period of life?

No. The infant brain is soft: as we grow older it becomes more consistent, and in old age acquires still greater firmness.

Does Phrenology apply solely to the human race?

It does not. The character of a dog is as much influenced by the form of its brain as that of a man.

If a large brain gives greater mental power than a small one, why is the brain of the sparrow inferior in size to that of the vulture, an animal greatly inferior in sagacity?

I answer this by stating that the circumstances in the two cases are by no means alike, and that we must compare the brains of animals of the same species before we can arrive at a proper knowledge of the effects of size. A large-brained vulture will manifest greater energy than a small-brained

GENERAL PRINCIPLES. 35

one, and so with the sparrow. It is evident that, in contrasting such different animals, circumstances are not the same, the organization or constitution of the sparrow's brain being different from that of the vulture's, and the intellectual organs relatively larger. Compare sparrows with sparrows, vultures with vultures, &c., and the truth of the phrenological maxim of size being, *cæteris paribus*, the index of power, will be made perfectly manifest. These remarks apply to the muscular system as well as to the brain—the bodily strength of some animals being much greater, in proportion to the size of their muscles than that of others of a different species. The flea, for example, as Haller has remarked, can draw from seventy to eighty times its own weight, whereas a horse cannot draw with ease more than three times its own weight. But of two fleas, that which has the larger muscles will have the greater strength. Again, some birds with small eyes have vision keener than birds of a different species with larger eyes. In every case, therefore, individuals of the same species must be compared.

Is intellectual power necessarily proportioned to the size of the brain as compared with that of the body?

It is not. The weight of the brain, for instance, to that of the body in man, (supposing him to weigh, on an average, 154 pounds) is about as 1 to 46; in several varieties of the ape tribe, as 1 to 22; in the sparrow, as 1 to 25; and in the canary, as 1 to 14. Man, therefore, has a smaller brain, in proportion to the size of his body, than any of these animals. In like manner, the brain of the sagacious elephant is relatively smaller than that of the goose; and the cerebral mass of the intelligent, half-reasoning dog, inferior in bulk to the brain of the cat, the rat, the mouse, and some other creatures far inferior in intellect. It thus appears, that in considering the intelligence of animals, we can ground little on the proportion subsisting between the brain and body.

Have all nations the same form of brain?

No. This varies considerably in different countries. The African brain differs in shape from the European, and so does the Carib and Esquimaux. Even in Europe, the same form of brain does not prevail rigidly; the German brain, for instance, is rounder and less elongated than the French.

Do dispositions ever change?

If the form and texture of the brain changes, so necessarily must the dispositions. The organ marked No. 1. in the bust, for example, is of late development, seldom attaining its full dimensions till the approach of manhood, when in consequence of its augmented growth a manifest change takes place in the character. The moral and intellectual organs also acquire a considerable increase about the same period. " It is now for the first time, that youth begin to feel strongly the impulse of moral sentiment, realize the force of moral obligation, and place a just estimate on moral conduct. Hence they are now recognised, in judicial proceedings, as moral agents. And hence, it is by no means uncommon for boys who had been previously vicious and unmanageable, to become now correct and docile."[17] If Mr Deville's experiments can be relied upon, we must infer that education and change of circumstances may alter the shape of the head. According to his observation, the change takes place in the situation of those organs the sphere of whose activity is increased or diminished.[18]

May not character change without a corresponding alteration in the shape of the head?

This in a limited sense is true. Circumstances by calling into activity organs which have been little exercised, or repressing the activity of others that have been much stimu-

[17] Phrenological Journal, vol. vii. p. 497.   [18] See Appendix, No. iv.

lated, may produce a change in the energy of their respective functions. Still, in such a case, the character is not radically different; it is only partially modified by the force of circumstances. Change these, and it will become as formerly.[19]

Can the dispositions of the lower animals be inferred from the form of their brain?

They can. Cruel ferocious animals, such as the tiger, and the hyena, have a particular form of brain very different from that possessed by gentle, timid creatures, as the fawn and the antelope. The brain of the hawk or vulture

---

[19] Supposing such men as Charlemagne and Richard Cœur de Lion, to have been apprenticed to a haberdasher, they would certainly cut no very distinguished figure in this situation; nay, it is more than probable, they would be dismissed on the score of negligence and dulness. Supposing, farther, that they are afterwards placed in situations calculated to call into play their great military talents, and that they become illustrious warriors, their former masters and fellow-shopmen would then call to mind the stupidity which they displayed behind the counter, and very gravely infer that a remarkable change has taken place in their characters. There is no such change, however, as is here imagined. While officiating as haberdashers, they were out of their element, and the formidable qualities of their minds had no room for display. When, however, it came to be a question of commanding armies, these qualities were brought into energetic operation, and they no longer appeared the same men. Dr. Blair has the following just remarks on change of character. "The seeds of various qualities, good and bad, lie in all our hearts; but until proper occasions ripen and bring them forward, they lie there inactive and dead." "For a while, the man is known neither by the world nor by himself to be what he truly is. But bring him into a new situation of life, which accords with his predominant dispositions, which strikes on certain latent qualities of his soul and awakens them into action; and as the leaves of a flower gradually unfold to the sun, so shall all his true character open full to view. This may, in one light be accounted, not so much an alteration of character, produced by a change of circumstances, as a discovery brought forth of the real character, which formerly lay concealed. Yet, at the same time, it is true that the man himself undergoes a change. For the opportunity being given for certain dispositions, which had been dormant, to exert themselves without restraint, they, of course, gather strength. By means of the ascendancy which they gain, other parts of the temper are borne down, and thus an alteration is made in the whole structure and system of the soul."—*Blair's Sermons.*

differs in shape from that of the dove. Birds which sing have a differently formed brain from those which do not.[20] A more accurate comparison, however, may be drawn between the heads of animals of the same species : thus, there is a marked difference in the heads of two horses or dogs, one gentle, and the other vicious.

What organs are we disposed to exercise most?

Those which are largest. Little gratification is experienced in the exercise of the weaker faculties : thus, a man who is not at all combative, would feel exceedingly annoyed at the idea of being obliged to fight ; while another, with a different configuration of brain would feel delight in having an opportunity of indulging his favourite propensity. Nor is this law confined to the cerebral organs : a man of great muscular power is fond of hard exercise ; another of little physical energy dislikes it, and is partial to rest.

Are the habitual attitude, expression, and language affected by the predominating organs ?

They generally are. It is seldom difficult to detect by his air, carriage, and conversation, when a man is proud, vain, bold, timid, or, crafty. These indications are called natural language, or pathognomy. Some persons deny its existence. When, however, we remind them that sighing, sobbing, and groaning are the natural language of grief; laughter of mirth; cursing and stamping with the foot of rage ; and trembling, paleness, and speechlessness of fear, they will see the absurdity of their denial. The existence of pathognomy, as connected with many of the faculties, is too obvious to require demonstration, and every man who has paid attention to the subject must admit it. By painters and actors it is acknowledged to the fullest extent. Who does not at once

---

[20] In many animals, however, we can draw no inference by looking at the head merely. In the elephant, for instance, an immense cavity or sinus intervenes betwixt the brain and the outer table of the skull.

recognize the strut of pride, the smirk of vanity, the compressed lip and energetic step of firmness, the stealthy glance of cunning, the upraised eye and lip of wonder, the bland expression and kindly tone of benevolence, the looks raised to heaven, the clasped hands, and bended knees of veneration!

Of how many organs does the brain consist?

It must consist of as many as there are primitive mental faculties. At present, phrenologists admit about thirty as distinctly established; others they speak of as probable; but these are not to be regarded as constituting the whole series. There are portions of the base of the brain whose functions are yet to be discovered.

Are the organs single or double?

As the brain is double, so is every organ; each has its fellow on the opposite side. There are thus, strictly speaking, about sixty organs ascertained, but as an organ on one side co-operates with its fellow on the other, it is customary to speak of the two as one, seeing that they manifest only a single mental quality.

May the brain be wounded or diseased on one side, and yet none of the mental faculties suspended?

Undoubtedly. If the organ of Tune, for instance, is injured on one side, its fellow on the other not being impaired, the faculty will continue to be manifested, although, as is natural to suppose, with less vigour than when both organs were perfectly sound; and the same law holds with regard to all the other organs, just as a person can still hear tolerably well with one ear, although the sense is quite lost in the other. But injury, of one side of the brain generally affects the other sympathetically; although the fact that it sometimes does not, and that the faculties go on not much impaired, is a sufficient proof both that there is a plurality of organs, and that the organs are double.[21]

---

[21] Careless observers often bring it as an argument against Phrenology

Are we always to expect a prominence or bump when a particular organ is large?

No. If several adjoining organs are all large, none of them will, probably, present any particular projection: there will be merely a general fulness in the locality occupied by them. It is only when an organ decidedly predominates over those in its immediate vicinity, that a protuberance is to be looked for. An inexperienced phrenologist has much difficulty in estimating the size of organs, where there is

that in cases of diseased brain, the mind is not at all affected, when some of its functions are in reality materially disordered. They perceive that the person, in common matters, acts perfectly well, that he answers questions intelligibly, and hence they conclude that every faculty is entire; whereas, if they were to investigate the matter more fully, and task the different organs severely, they would perceive in the manifestations of some of them a considerable falling off. The above argument, supposing it to be valid, would only go to prove that the mind has no connexion with the brain, a proposition so absurd that no sane intellect can now for a moment entertain it; but why should the argument bear more against Phrenology, which teaches that each faculty of the mind is manifested by a particular part of the brain, than against the opposite doctrine that the whole brain is concerned in the manifestation of each faculty? Cases of extensive disease of the lungs and liver are occasionally met with, where respiration and the biliary secretion are very little affected. In the number for July, 1833, of the Glasgow Medical Journal, we are told of a case in the Stirling Dispensary where six pounds of fluid were found in the right cavity of the chest, compressing the corresponding lung into a mere membrane, a fourth of an inch in thickness; and yet during life, breathing, though a little hurried, appeared to be fully and perfectly performed, and the man had no symptoms which indicated in the most remote degree the existence of thoracic disease. What would we think if, from such a case, it was attempted to be inferred that the lungs were not the organs of respiration. Admirably in this instance as the sound lung supplied the part of the diseased one, still it is not to be inferred that the respiratory apparatus was capable of sustaining the same effort as in perfect health. For ordinary breathing it sufficed almost perfectly, but had the person attempted running or any other violent exercise, its inadequacy would then have appeared sufficiently manifest. The same remark applies to the brain. In injuries thereof, when the intellect is said not to suffer, we must ascertain whether the part injured is really connected with the intellect. It may appertain to the propensities or sentiments, in which case the intellectual powers may not suffer, although the injury is considerable.

uniformity of surface, and is hence apt to deny the possibility of practically following up the science; but one who has sufficiently studied it feels no such difficulty. He estimates the dimensions of the organs correctly, although there is not the slightest bulging out of any particular part beyond those in its vicinity ; but this requires considerable experience, and is not to be learned all at once.

Does Phrenology admit of exceptions?

It does not. A single exception would entirely overthrow whatever part of the phrenological doctrine it should be at variance with. When an apparent exception does occur, it must be attributed to ignorance on the part of the observer, or to a want of health in the brain. Taking mankind in the mass, a skilful phrenologist will infer character with great accuracy in nineteen cases out of twenty. It is not pretended, however, that practical Phrenology has yet attained to perfection.[22]

How are the faculties classified?

The faculties are divided into two orders—the FEELINGS,

---

[22] The reputation of Phrenology has been often endangered by the abortive attempts of ignorant pretenders to infer character from examination of the head. Before this can be done properly, not only much experience, but a good share of tact and analytical talent are necessary. There are two risks to be encountered, that of estimating erroneously the size of the different organs, and that of drawing faulty conclusions from the estimate, even supposing it to be true. Spurzheim was strongly opposed to the practice, now so much in vogue, of indiscriminately inferring character from examination of the head. Where the character is a marked one, the science may be benefited by observing how far the talents and dispositions correspond with the form of brain possessed by the individual; but how seldom is it that we meet with marked characters ! These observations are the more necessary, as there are a set of phrenological quacks, who, on all occasions, undertake to tell the character of any person, however common-place. Such pretenders naturally fall into errors, and an outcry is immediately raised that Phrenology is false. With the same reason might it be said, that there is no truth in Davy's allegation that the alkalies possess metallic bases, because the fact could not be demonstrated experimentally by some bungler in Chemistry.

or AFFECTIVE FACULTIES, and the INTELLECT. These, again, are divided into Genera—the FEELINGS into the *Propensities* and *Sentiments*, and the INTELLECT into the *Perceptive* and *Reflective Faculties*. This arrangement is not unobjectionable, but in the present state of our knowledge, a perfectly accurate classification of the faculties cannot be attained.

ORDER I.—FEELINGS OR AFFECTIVE FACULTIES.

What are the feelings, or affective faculties?

They may be described simply as those faculties which give rise to affections or emotions, and which neither know nor reason. They are, in themselves, mere blind impulses, and unless governed by the intellect are apt to run into the grossest abuses. Thus Destructiveness, without such guidance, may lead to indiscriminate violence and massacre, Veneration to the worshipping of images instead of the true God, Adhesiveness to attachment to worthless characters, Self-Esteem to exorbitant pride, and Love of Approbation to overweening and ridiculous vanity.

GENUS I.—PROPENSITIES.

What is a propensity?

The term Propensity, is applied by Dr. Spurzheim, to those affective faculties which produce only desires or inclinations, and which likewise prompt to certain corresponding modes of action. The classification of the faculties, however, is not altogether in accordance with this definition.

1. AMATIVENESS.

Where is this organ situated, and what is its function?

The cerebellum, or little brain, which lies in the lower and posterior portion of the skull, immediately under the cerebrum, or brain proper, and behind the top of the spinal marrow is the seat of the amative propensity. This point is now universally admitted by physiologists, and is supported by so many facts that it can no longer be doubtful. The effects of cerebellar disease in calling the sexual feeling

AMATIVENESS.

into vehement action, demonstrate conclusively that the latter has its seat in the particular part of brain alluded to. The great purpose served by Amativeness is the continuance of the species.[23]

What external indications are presented when the organ is very large?

There is much fulness at the back and lower part of the head, an unusual distance between the mastoid processes,[24] and great thickness of the neck. Subjoined is an engraving of the Emperor Caracalla's head, in which the rotundity and thickness of neck, and its extent backwards from the ear will be observed. It represents a very great development of the organ in question.

[23] The circumstances which led Dr. Gall to the discovery of the organ are curious, and are fully detailed in his own great work, and in the writings of Dr. Spurzheim.

[24] Those hard prominences immediately behind, and at the root of the ear.

Is the organ larger in men than in the other sex?

It is so in most cases. Women in whom it is large, are more easily seduced than those with a small development: it is generally very full in those unfortunate females who walk the streets, and gain a livelihood by prostitution. In what are called "ladies' men" the organ is small. These individuals feel towards women precisely as they would to one of their own sex. Women intuitively know this, and acquire a kind of easy familiarity with them which they do not attain with men of a warmer complexion.[25]

In what state is the organ at different periods of life?

In childhood it is very small, not only absolutely but relatively. At birth, the cerebellum to the rest of the brain is as 1 to 13, 15, or 20. In adults as 1 to 6, 7, or 8. In some, however, it is much less. The organ increases rapidly on the approach of manhood, and at this period, dull pains are often experienced in the site of it. In old age, it diminishes, like the rest of the brain, but in a greater ratio.[26]

---

25 Ladies' men have small heads. Self-Esteem is usually small, and Love of Approbation well developed. A large brain, especially if Self-Esteem is also large, unfits a man for performing the character successfully.

26 "By the kindness" of Baron Larrey, says Dr. Gall, "I saw a soldier whose antipathy to women degenerated into perfect madness. The sight of a woman threw him into fits and rendered him almost furious. Dr. Spurzheim has seen a similar circumstance in England. In each of these individuals the cerebellum was exceedingly small. A physician of Vienna, whose talents were of a high order, showed a marked antipathy to women, a peculiarity which, at the time, we attributed to his love of solitude. Some years afterwards he died of phthisis, and, in his otherwise large head, the space appropriated for the cerebellum was extremely small. The distance from one mastoid process to the other was scarcely three inches: the occipital cavities instead of bulging out were partly quite flat, partly even depressed." "It has been objected that an organ cannot produce an effect opposite to that of its functions; but is not the stomach the organ of appetite and does it not sometimes happen that, in consequence of a weak state of this viscus, we have a disgust at any kind of food?"

When does the organ attain its full size?

In the male, between the ages of eighteen and twenty-six; in the female a little earlier. Young lads are generally indifferent about female society, and young girls about that of men. As the organ in question, enlarges, a change is produced in the feelings of the two sexes, and they become fond of associating with each other. Women with small Amativeness and large Adhesiveness prefer the society of their own sex to that of men. To the latter their manners seem passionless and frigid; and even when gifted with beauty, they are felt by the opposite sex to be far less interesting than women to whom nature has granted fewer charms of person but a different cerebral conformation.

What does celibacy generally result from?

In general, from a small development of this organ, with moderate Adhesiveness and Philoprogenitiveness. Persons so constituted, even although they can conveniently do so, rarely marry. Judging from the portraits of Kant, Newton, and Charles XII., the organ of Amativeness seems to have been small in the heads of these illustrious men, and the strength of the faculty is understood to have been in keeping with this feeble development. The same remark applies to the Right Hon. William Pitt.[27]

Is there any thing particular in the action of this organ, as respects the inferior animals?

There is. In most of them it is periodically excited; being at other times in a great measure inactive.

[27] "Some opponents of the phrenological doctrine affirm, that physical love has been found very strong in individuals who have possessed a very small cerebellum, or in whom that organ was more or less completely destroyed. I am doubtful how far facts of this kind merit confidence. As for myself, I declare that I cannot admit them until they shall have been seen by phrenologists; we must look with particular caution on facts which are only witnessed by the enemies of a system, especially when we know to what lengths designing persons are capable of pushing their falsehoods."— *Broussais.*

2. PHILOPROGENITIVENESS.

Describe the locality of this organ.

It lies immediately above Amativeness, in the middle of the occiput, and, when large, gives a drooping appearance to the back of the head, which projects much, and hangs, as it were, over the neck. A large development of the organ is shown in the following sketch.

What is its function?

To bestow an ardent attachment to offspring, and children in general; and, according to some phrenologists, to weak and tender animals.

In which sex is it larger?

In the female; and this law extends to the lower animals as well as to our own race. Boys exhibit little of it; the case is different with little girls, who show its activity in their fondness for dolls, and in their desire to carry children in their arms, even when they can scarcely stand under their weight. Mary Wolstoncroft denies that girls have, by nature, a greater fondness for dolls than boys, ascribing the difference to education; but she is clearly mistaken, inasmuch as the organ on which the love of young depends, is decidedly larger in the female head than in the male. The fondness of unmarried women, or married women who are childless, for cats and lap-dogs, seems to depend chiefly upon this organ.

In which of the lower animals is it peculiarly large?

In the monkey tribe, whose affection for their young is quite remarkable. It was the size of the organ in these creatures, coupled with their love of offspring, which led Dr. Gall to suspect the faculty to be connected with this portion of the brain.

Do all animals display love of offspring?

No. The cuckoo (both male and female) abandons its offspring, and leaves them to be brought up by other birds. Many male animals take no charge whatever of their young, while others do so conjointly with the females. Such is the case with the fox, the wolf, the roebuck, the rabbit, and various others.

Does love of children not rather proceed from general benevolence?

No; for persons who have little of this virtue are often passionately fond of children, and others who have a great deal of it care not for their society. The most ferocious savages are often extremely affectionate towards their children. Burke the murderer had a large development of this organ, and was very fond of children, and beloved by them in return.

What is the result of a small development?

Indifference to children. It is a great evil when a mother is so constituted; for, however estimable she may otherwise be, she will find the rearing of her offspring a toil rather than a pleasure; and, unless her conscientiousness and prudence be great, she will be very apt to neglect them. No woman will make a good nurse unless well endowed with this organ. Women who commit infanticide have generally a small development.[28]

What is the result of a great development?

An ardent love of children. The person delights to take them on his knee, to kiss them, to relate stories to them, to play with them, &c. Some of the sternest minds and greatest heroes have been distinguished for the strength of this feeling. Agesilaus, the warlike monarch of Sparta, used to ride on a stick to please his children. On one occasion, King Henry IV. of France was seen galloping on all fours, one of his children on his back, and the other flogging him with a whip. The passion must have been very strong in these illustrious men. Children have an intuitive know-

---

[28] Dr. Spurzheim has examined thirty-seven child-murderers, and in thirty of them the organ of Philoprogenitiveness was very small. "In women," says he, "as well as in the females of animals, this propensity has different degrees of energy. Certain cows do not suffer their calves to suck; some pigs, cats, rabbits, &c. kill their young, while other females of the same kind of animals cry for several days, and refuse to eat, when they are bereft of their offspring. It is a lamentable truth that this difference of motherly love exists also in mankind. All women do not desire to become mothers; some consider their pregnancy as the greatest misfortune. Several mothers seek various pretexts in order to remove their children out of the house. There are others who, being freed from shame, reproach, misery, and many inconveniences, by the loss of their illegitimate children, yet shed tears for a long time after, at the remembrance of them. Others, on the contrary, see their legitimate offspring buried without a pang. Thus, it is beyond doubt that natural love of offspring is very weak in some women. It is, therefore, wrong to believe that infanticide is a more unnatural act than any other murder."—*View of the Elementary Principles of Education,* 2d edit. p. 319.

ledge of persons in whom this organ is large, and come to them, as it were, instinctively.[29]

What are the abuses likely to result from too great a development of Philoprogenitiveness?

If the feeling be excessive, and not regulated by the influence of other faculties, the children will be apt to get spoiled, and become pert, noisy, unmannerly, and self-willed. Philoprogenitiveness sometimes becomes diseased, and then there is the most violent love of offspring, with overwhelming grief, often terminating in madness, at their loss.

3. CONCENTRATIVENESS.

Where is Concentrativeness situated?

It lies immediately above Philoprogenitiveness, and below Self-Esteem.

What purpose is served by this organ?

It is believed by the leading Scotch phrenologists to be the seat of that power which enables us to direct the intellect continuously to a particular subject of thought. Persons with a large endowment are not apt to be distracted from what they are engaged in, by the intrusion of extraneous ideas. When the organ is disproportionately large or active, absence of mind, or abstraction, is the result.

When deficient, what is the consequence?

The individual is remarkable for great volatility of manner, and extreme difficulty in directing his mind, for a length of time, towards any one subject. He is continually flying

---

[29] Dr. Gall justly observes, that if in men who have an ardent love of children, "the organ of Amativeness is feebly developed, they console themselves for the loss of a beloved spouse with a resignation which appears very philosophical, while the death of a child plunges them into long-continued and inconsolable grief. The barrenness of their wives distresses them exceedingly, and often leads them to treat with coldness, women who are otherwise unexceptionable."

from topic to topic, and finds it almost impossible to pursue a continued train of investigation. Scatter-brained, flighty people, are all deficient in Concentrativeness. Good abilities may exist, however, along with this deficiency, but in such a case they are deprived of half their usefulness and effect.

Has it the same power over all the faculties?

Probably not; it appears to act more influentially on some than on others. I conceive, that the faculties concerned in reasoning and calculation, are, in an especial manner, governed by it; hence metaphysicians, mathematicians, &c., are peculiarly subject to mental absence.

Are phrenologists agreed on the functions of this organ?

No. Dr. Spurzheim conceived it to be the source of attachment to particular places; hence he called it Inhabitiveness.[30] He never coincided with the views of the Scotch phrenologists, and by both parties the subject is left open for farther investigation.

Mention a few authors whose writings are distinguished by Concentrativeness.

Campbell, Pope, and Byron, all display a vigorous concentration of thought and style. In Scott, Coleridge, and Southey, there is much less. We may infer (supposing us to have properly localised this faculty) a great development of the organ of Concentrativeness in such men as Tacitus, Thucydides, Reid, Locke, and Brown, and less in Dugald

---

[30] *Amor patriæ* was supposed by Dr. Spurzheim to result from Inhabitiveness, but I have never been able to see, that one organ is necessary to give attachment to places, and another to give attachment to persons. The question has often been asked, Why are mountaineers more ardent patriots than the inhabitants of the plains? Supposing the fact to be true, we are not justified in inferring, that the former are patriots merely because they happen to be mountaineers; for the real cause may be, that they are secluded, and have little opportunity of getting their views expanded into cosmopolitanism. The more the intellect is enlightened, the less vivid does that ardent attachment to one's *natale solum*, which often constitutes patriotism, become. Savages are the most attached to their native land.

Stewart and Beattie. Archimedes, Newton, and Adam Smith, must have possessed the faculty in vast energy.

4. ADHESIVENESS.

Describe the situation and function of this organ.

It lies at each side of, and rather above, Philoprogenitiveness, and is that portion of the brain with which the feeling of attachment is connected. No faculty, save Destructiveness, is displayed more early than this: it is exhibited even by the infant in the nurse's arms. When very strong, it gives ardent strength of attachment and warmth of friendship.

Does this faculty constitute love?

Not strictly speaking; for love, in the legitimate sense of the word, is a compound of Amativeness and Adhesiveness. Such is the love which the lover bears to his mistress, and the husband to his young wife. The attachment of a parent to his child, or of a brother to his sister, is not, in reality, love, but strong Adhesiveness—powerfully aided, in the former case, by Philoprogenitiveness.

Is this faculty more energetic in men or women?

Generally in the latter;[31] although in men there are not

---

[31] " Women are generally more devoted to their friends than men, and display an indefatigable activity in serving them. Whoever has gained the affection of a woman is sure to succeed in any enterprise wherein she assists him: men draw back much sooner in such cases. Frequently in my life, have I had occasion to admire in females the most generous zeal on behalf of their friends. Who is not astonished at the courage shown by a woman when her husband, whose misconduct has perhaps a thousand times offended her, is threatened with imminent danger? Who does not know many instances of the most heroic devotedness on the part of the sex? A woman spares no effort to serve her friend When it is a question of saving her brother, her husband, her father, she penetrates into prisons—she throws herself at the feet of her sovereign. Such are the women of our day, and such has history represented those of antiquity. Happy, I repeat, is he who has a woman for a friend!"—*Gall.*

wanting instances of the most violent attachments, even towards their own sex. Such is represented to have been the case with Pylades and Orestes, and with Damon and Pythias, whose attachment to each other (the result of excessive Adhesiveness) defied even death itself. What beautiful pictures of friendship between men, have been drawn by Homer, by Virgil, and by the sacred writers, in the instances of Achilles and Patroclus, of Nisus and Euryalus, and of Jonathan and David!

Can this faculty co-exist with small Benevolence?

Facts prove that it may. Robbers and murderers sometimes display such wonderful attachment to each other, that even the rack has failed to extort from them the names of their accomplices in crime. Mary M'Innes, who was executed for murder, had a large development of this organ, and displayed its function with great energy on the scaffold. Friendship, however, is destitute of much of its lustre, when the moral and intellectual sentiments have not the predominance in the mind. A warm friend may then easily be converted into a mischievous foe.

Is it subject to abuse?

Very frequently it is so. Young women, and sometimes young men, are apt to form absurd and romantic attachments to each other, which, however, being based upon an unnatural state of excitement in the organ of Adhesiveness, necessarily terminate so soon as the excitement ends; and thus, unless there are eminent moral qualities to ensure permanence, the feeling is seldom of long duration. When a coldness once takes place, mutual antipathy often follows, and the quondam friends become bitter enemies. People labouring under the strong influence of this organ, are often incapable of perceiving any thing like blemish in their friends. They clothe them with the attributes of perfection, and employ the most extravagant terms of praise when speaking of them to others. Clanship, when improperly directed, and attachment to worthless characters, are abuses of the faculty.

What is the natural language of Adhesiveness?

There is a tendency to turn the head, in the direction of the organ, towards the object to whom we are attached. Young girls may be seen coming from school with their arms thrown over each other's neck, and the sides of the head meeting just at the seat of this organ. A mother fondling her child, turns the side of her head towards it. Two lovers taking a walk arm in arm, incline the head mutually in the same way.

5. COMBATIVENESS.

Where is this organ situated?

Between the mastoid process and the organs of Philoprogenitiveness and Adhesiveness. It corresponds to the inferior angle of the parietal bone, and lies immediately behind, and on a level with, the top of the ear.

In what manner does the faculty manifest itself?

In a love of opposition and strife. It gives boldness to the character. The combative man loves danger, meets it fearlessly, and triumphs over difficulties, which would overwhelm a person in whom the organ was feebly developed.

In what class of men is the organ large?

It is invariably large in great heroes, in determined prize-fighters, and in men any way remarkable for active courage. The gladiators of Rome must have been largely endowed with it.[32] It is remarkably prominent in the skulls of King Robert Bruce and General Wurmser who were both pre-eminent

---

[32] The statues of the gladiators display an ample bulging out in the seat of the organ—a proof that the ancients recognized great courage to exist in combination with a particular form of head. This, of itself, is a striking evidence of the correctness of the locality assigned to the organ by phrenologists.

for valour. It was very large in the head of the French General Lamarque, whose courage was remarkable, and appears greatly developed in the likenesses of Duguesclin, another French warrior, distinguished for his extraordinary valour. In the skull of Robert Burns it is very large; which accounts, in some measure, for his controversial propensities. It was amply developed in Dr. Gall who possessed, in a great degree, the quality of personal courage. The character of Balfour of Burley, as delineated in "Old Mortality," is a remarkable instance of Combativeness, Destructiveness, and Firmness, all greatly developed. The same remark applies to the character of Charles the Bold, as displayed in "Quentin Durward." The history of Murat, and of Marshal Ney, "the bravest of the brave," presents in great perfection the picture of excessive Combativeness. The organ, when large, is easily discriminated.

If we compare such a head as that of Duguesclin, in the above engraving, with that of a person who dislikes fighting or contention, a marked difference of shape will be perceived in the position of the organ.

Is a man with much Combativeness necessarily addicted to fighting or other varieties of contention?

Such is the natural tendency of his mind, although, in common circumstances, he may, by means of other faculties, keep this one sufficiently under restraint. If Destructiveness is moderate and Benevolence large, some kind of harmless contention will be preferred. The former organ, however, is very generally large when Combativeness is well developed.

Are all nations equally endowed with this faculty?

No. The organ is small in the Hindoo and Peruvian heads, and exceedingly large in the Carib; and the dispositions of these nations are in perfect accordance with their respective developments—the two former being mild and unwarlike, the latter immoderately fond of fighting.

What happens when the organ is too large, or not sufficiently controlled by others?

The consequences are lamentable. The individual is for ever engaged in quarrels and getting himself involved in difficulties, from his ungovernable love of contention. Should Destructiveness be also full, he is very apt to strike on any occasion in which he may be offended. " A word and a blow " is his favourite maxim. He is a profound admirer of the *argumentum ad hominem.*

What is the result when the organ is very small?

In such a case, the person abhors strife and competition of every kind, and purposely avoids them. His temper may be warm, but he will seldom have courage to display it in the form of blows.

Is Combativeness a useful faculty?

It is eminently so, by conferring determination and intrepidity of character. " Courage," says Dr. Johnson, " is a quality so necessary for maintaining virtue, that it is always respected, even when it is associated with vice."

Are the consequences of a large development as strongly marked in the lower animals as in man?

They are. The poodle, the pointer, and the spaniel have the organ small, the bull dog and the mastiff large; and the dispositions of the animals correspond. " Dogs," observes Dr. Gall, " that cannot be trained for fighting, have the head narrow above, and a little behind the ears; while those possessed of much courage are large in this region." In the heads of the two dogs represented in the section on Benevolence, the difference of size in the region of Combativeness is very apparent. Cock-fighters and pigeon-fanciers know from experience, that a particular formation of head in these birds is connected with courage, and another with cowardice. This difference exists in the region of Combativenes.

6. DESTRUCTIVENESS.

What quality results from this organ?

The passion to destroy, and the propensity to inflict pain, uneasiness, and injury in general. When uncontrolled by Benevolence it prompts to unmitigated cruelty, and the person is fierce, passionate, revengeful, and ferocious. When so controlled, there is merely much warmth of feeling, irascibility without cruelty, and a tendency to be severe on proper occasions.

How is a large Destructiveness known?

By a considerable and rounded fulness above the opening of the ear, and by width of head at that part. Those whose heads are flat in this situation, and narrow above the ears, are never destructive. When the external opening of the ear is placed very low, it is one sign of large Destructiveness. The skull delineated in the engraving exhibits a remarkably large development of this organ. It belonged to an incorrigible female thief, of whom Dr. Gall observes, that a case will never be met with, in which the organs, whose abuse leads to theft, to cunning, and to murder, are more amply developed.

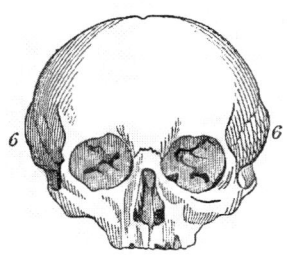

How was the organ first ascertained?

Dr. Gall first noticed it by observing the difference at this particular situation, between the heads of carnivorous and graminivorous animals. In the former the quantity of brain in the region of Destructiveness is great; in the latter the reverse.[33]

When does Destructiveness first display itself?

At the moment of birth. The angry cries of the newborn child are manifestations of the faculty.[34]

Does a large development communicate any particular character to the manner and expression?

Yes: destructive people have generally a sharp, sparkling

---

[33] All carnivorous animals are necessarily destructive. Some of them, such as the wolf, the fox, the bear, and the lion, kill only to procure food, others from a mere blind pleasure in killing, as is the case with the tiger, the hyena, the pole-cat, the marten, and the weasel.

[34] An irritable frame is favourable to the activity of Destructiveness; hence the frequent ebullitions of temper displayed during the reign of childhood, and also by grown people who labour under bad health. "No man," says Lord Bacon, "is angry, who feels not himself hurt: and, therefore, delicate and tender persons must needs be often angry, they have so many things to trouble them, which more robust natures have little sense of."

eye, a loud and often cutting voice, quickness of movement, and energy of character. When engaged in disputation, they are apt to get fierce and animated, striking the table, as if to enforce their positions, and speaking in a loud and irritated manner.[35]

In what class of persons may a large development be expected?

Distinguished warriors, duellists, sportsmen, and boxers, and severe and sarcastic polemics must be well endowed with the organ; so must surgeons who are passionately fond of operations, and men who, from choice, follow the trade of a butcher. In such men as Knox and Luther, it, in combination with Combativeness, must have been large. It was very large in the head of King Robert Bruce. It prompts and gives keenness to satire, and is very perceptible in the style of such writers as Pope, Burns, Byron, Swift, and Smollett. In the heads of the murderers Hare, Burke, and Bellingham, it was large, and it must have been excessive in those of Nero, Caligula, Marat, Danton, and Robespièrre.[36]

May a virtuous man have this organ as largely developed as a murderer?

He may undoubtedly, but in him there are other faculties which keep it in check, and prevent the display of its more violent manifestations; the murderer has no such restraints.

---

[35] The frequent indulgence in Destructiveness gives coarseness of manners. " Whence," as Lord Kaimes inquires, " the rough and harsh manners of our West India planters, but from the unrestrained license of venting ill-humour upon their negro slaves ?"

[36] Calvin, who burned Servetus over a slow fire, for differing with him on a point of theology, must have had a large endowment of this organ. Both Combativeness and Destructiveness appear very large in the portraits of Bonner, Bishop of London, a man of violent charater, and coarse both in his manners and language, and who, during the reign of the " Bloody " Mary, consigned to the flames no fewer than 200 individuals for their religious opinions. Caliban, in Shakspeare's play of " The Tempest," is an incarnation of pure Destructiveness.

DESTRUCTIVENESS.

The late Dr. Gregory, and Mr. Abernethy, the distinguished and eccentric surgeon, had probably as great a development of Destructiveness, absolutely speaking, as Bellingham; but in them it was controlled by energetic moral and intellectual faculties ; while the miserable assassin of Perceval being wofully deficient in these, was left to the unbridled sway of his lower propensities, and revelled in vice. Thus, although the positive size of Destructiveness may not have been greater in him than in them, yet its relative magnitude in proportion to the organs of the moral feelings, was infinitely greater, and hence the criminal tendencies of his depraved mind.

How do you reconcile the good endowment of Benevolence possessed by Thurtell, with his character as a murderer ?

Thurtell frequently showed traits of benevolent feeling, and was, on this account, rather popular with his associates. His Benevolence, however, was no match for the excited energy of his great Destructiveness, and other animal propensities ; and a phrenologist, on examining his head, so far from inferring it to be that of an amiable or virtuous character would conclude that it belonged to one strongly addicted to low indulgences, and, when in a state of excitement, to acts of violent outrage. When the propensities were not in this excited condition, he would manifest good-nature and benevolence, and the annals of his life show that he was very capable of kind actions.[37] It is Phrenology alone

---

[37] Some people foolishly imagine, that when a man is hanged for taking away life, he must needs be totally destitute of Benevolence; not reflecting that people are always governed by the strongest motives, and that if, in an unhappy moment, Destructiveness is so furiously excited, as to overpower the counteracting effect of Benevolence, it must lead to violent, and frequently fatal, results. Had Thurtell possessed a very poor development of Benevolence, his head would have afforded a strong argument that phrenologists were in error respecting the locality of this organ, in so far as, in accordance with such a development, his whole actions should have been characterized by a destitution of benevolent feeling, which was very far from being the case. Moir, who was executed for shooting, in a fit of

which can explain these apparent anomalies of character. Men of far higher moral powers than Thurtell, have been hanged for murder, committed in a moment of violent passion, under the influence of a provoked and ungovernable Destructiveness.[38]

Mention a few modes in which the feeling manifests itself.
It is shown in a love of hunting, rat-killing, dog-fighting,

---

violent passion, a fisherman who had grossly insulted and outraged him, was understood to be a very benevolent man, when his ungovernable temper was not roused into activity. It would be absurd to expect, in such a head, a small organ of Benevolence, and yet he was hanged for murder. A man was executed in Glasgow, a few years ago, for stabbing a person by whom he was overpowered, in a fight which took place between them when half drunk. This man's previous character was not only fair, but excellent. Mackean, who was hanged at Glasgow for the murder of the Lanark carrier, had a pretty fair Benevolence, and, till the commission of this crime, his character displayed traits of the feeling, and was not considered very bad. He perpetrated the deed in a momentary fit of rage, and his Destructiveness was such as would prompt to violence under provocation. Had Benevolence been small, the general tenor of his life would have indicated its feeble influence, but such was not the case. A good development of this organ, with preponderating Destructiveness and Combativeness, deficient Conscientiousness, and a poor intellect, especially if the person moves in depraved society, and is addicted to drinking, will not secure him against the commission of gross violence, and, under certain circumstances, of murder itself.

[38] Peter the Great was a striking illustration of Benevolence and Destructiveness—of kindness and cruelty in combination. " Owing to the circumstances in which he was placed, and the determination to execute the plan he had conceived of remodelling the customs and institutions of his country, he had to maintain a constant struggle between his good and evil genius. Nothing was too great, nothing too little for his comprehensive mind. The noblest undertakings were mixed with the most farcical amusements; the most laudable institutions for the benefit of his subjects were followed by shaving their beards and docking their skirts. Kind-hearted, benevolent, and humane, he set no value on human life. Owing to these, and many other incongruities, his character has necessarily been represented in various points of view, and in various colours by his biographers." " His memory among his countrymen, who ought to be the best judges, and of whom he was at once the scourge and the benefactor, is held in the highest veneration."—*Family Library*.

and attending public executions. It is told of La Condamine, that on one occasion, when he was making efforts to penetrate the crowd assembled to witness an execution, and was pushed back by the soldiers, the executioner said, "Let the gentleman pass, he is an amateur." The mischievous habit of breaking windows, gates, posts, and trees, so common in this country, is a manifestation of the faculty: so is the common and atrocious crime of fire-raising. A passionate child kicks the stool over which it stumbled : this simple act proceeds from Destructiveness. People who indulge in abuse are all destructive. Cursing and swearing are displays of the propensity. Xantippe, the wife of Socrates, was highly destructive, so was Catherine, in the comedy of "The Taming of the Shrew," and so is the whole family of scolds and termagants. Clergymen who address themselves much to the fears of their audience, and dwell strongly upon the terrors of future punishment, have this organ large.

Is Destructiveness often violently roused?

No organ is so frequently in a state of excitation. You cannot cross the street, or sit an hour in the company of people of different religious or political sentiments, without seeing it called into action. If you behold a cat pouncing upon a mouse, or two dogs growling at each other about a bone, you have an instance of the faculty being at work. Homicidal monomania, or the irresistible desire to murder, is the effect of a diseased excitement of Destructiveness, and many miserable lunatics have perished on the scaffold, for homicides committed under its influence. Great ignorance prevails among judges and juries with regard to this subject.[39]

---

[39] I saw a man, named Papavoine, guillotined at Paris, in 1825, for murder. On reading his trial, I was strongly impressed with the idea that the crime was committed under the influence of insanity, and that the man ought not to have been put to death. This view of the case has been since adopted in works on insanity, and is now admitted to be sound. The same year, I

Are destructive people necessarily brave?

No. They are often great cowards when brought to face real danger. Valour depends upon Combativeness, and destructive people have often little of this quality. At the same time, Destructiveness sharpens Combativeness, and adds much to its energy on the field of battle. Firmness gives endurance to both these faculties, and prevents them from rapidly exhausting themselves.[40]

What results from a want of Destructiveness?

The mind is deficient in fire and edge, and in that degree of severity which is of great use in the business of life.

---

witnessed at Versailles, the decapitation of a miserable wretch, convicted of murdering, and of afterwards eating the flesh of his victim—a young girl, against whom he entertained no animosity whatever. When apprehended, he had plenty of money upon him, a proof that he was not impelled by want. He could assign no motive for the dreadful act, but an insatiable desire to eat human flesh. Gaulius speaks of a man who had a similar passion, and who, to gratify it, committed many murders. His daughter, though separated from him, and well brought up, yielded to the same horrible desire, and became also a cannibal. "At the commencement of the last century," says Spurzheim, "many murders were committed in Holland, upon the frontiers of Cleves. The author of these crimes was, for a long time, unknown, but at last an old musician, who was in the habit of playing the violin at all the weddings in the neighbourhood, was suspected, in consequence of some remarks which escaped his children. Being brought before a magistrate, he acknowledged thirty-four murders, and declared that he committed them without animosity, or wish to rob, but simply because he felt therein an extraordinary degree of pleasure." The whole of these persons were, unquestionably, monomaniacs.

[40] A man is met on the highway by a robber, who presents a pistol to his breast, and demands his money. If the man is greatly endowed with Firmness, but deficient in Combativeness, he will sternly refuse to surrender his purse, but do nothing more. If he possesses, along with Firmness, a great deal of Combativeness, he will be inclined to rush forward, and wrench the weapon from the hand of his assailant. Here the function of Combativeness will cease; but supposing the individual to be largely endowed with Destructiveness also, he will endeavour to knock the aggressor down, to punish him with severity, and perhaps kill him on the spot. In most persons, Destructiveness is large enough to give rise to such manifestations in the circumstances supposed.

† ALIMENTIVENESS.

What is meant by this term ?

Alimentiveness is the name applied to one of the organs, not yet regarded as fully ascertained : it is supposed to be connected with the desire for food. In the bust, it bears no number, but is marked † ; it lies in front of, and a little above, the opening of the ear. Farther observations are necessary, to determine finally whether the function assigned to this part of the brain be correct; but many facts render this highly probable.

How does it display itself when very large?

It is supposed to do so in an inordinate fondness for indulging in the pleasures of the table. If this belief is correct, gluttons and epicures ought to be well endowed with the organ, and probably drunkards also. Indeed, Dr. Caldwell of Lexington, in his ingenious " Thoughts on Intemperance,"[41] conceives the habit of drunkenness to depend upon a highly excited state of this organ, and proposes to cure it by means of local applications, tending to diminish high action in the brain. It is certain that, by nature, some people are much more addicted to eating and drinking than others, and it can hardly be doubted, that these propensities depend upon a special organ. The abuses of the faculty are gluttony and drunkenness.[42]

---

[41] Published in the Transylvania Journal of Medicine, July, &c. 1832. See also the Phrenological Journal, vol. viii. p. 624.

[42] In the Journal of the Phrenological Society of Paris, the case of a woman called Denise, detailed in the " Annales de la Médecine Physiologique," (October, 1832) is taken notice of, as furnishing a curious example of insatiable appetite for food. In infancy, she exhausted the milk of all her nurses, and ate four times more than other children of the same age. At school, she devoured the bread of all the scholars; and in the Salpêtrière it was found impossible to satisfy her habitual appetite with less than eight or ten pounds of bread daily. Nevertheless, she there experi-

LOVE OF LIFE.

Does the love of existence depend upon a particular organ?
It is so conjectured by phrenologists, who conceive that a portion of the lower and inner side of the middle lobe of the brain is probably the seat of this feeling. Facts, however, are more deficient here, than even with regard to the organ of Alimentiveness. There is much reason to suppose that Love of Life depends upon a special organ, for we do not always find that those whose lot has been most fortunately cast, as respects riches, health, and other things considered worth living for, set the highest value upon existence. The wretched and half-starved mendicant often dreads the termination of life more than the happy and the prosperous, and this altogether without any reference to a future state and its punishments. Dr. Johnson had an extreme terror of death: if this feeling has a special organ, it must have been large in him. Dr. Thomas Brown treats of " the desire of continued existence " as a special faculty.

enced, two or three times a month, great attacks of hunger, during which she devoured twenty-four pounds of bread daily. If, during these fits, any obstacle was opposed to the gratification of her imperious desire, she became so furious that she used to bite her clothes, and even hands, and did not recover her reason till hunger was completely satisfied. Being one day in the kitchen of a rich family, where a dinner party was expected, she devoured, in a very few minutes, the soup intended for twenty guests, along with twelve pounds of bread. On another occasion, she drank all the coffee prepared for seventy-five of her companions in the Salpétrière! Her skull is small; the region of the propensities predominates.

In the head of the semi-idiot, Barclay, executed for murder, the organ of Alimentiveness was very large, and the excessive craving for food corresponded. He clamoured for it shortly before being brought upon the scaffold, and on the morning of his execution ate a breakfast which would have sufficed for three healthy men.

For an account of all that is at present known concerning this organ, see an excellent article, by Mr. Robert Cox, in the Phrenological Journal, vol. x. p. 249.

7. SECRETIVENESS.

Describe the seat and tendency of this organ.

Secretiveness is situated immediately above Destructiveness, as may be seen by referring to the bust. When the latter organ is very large, and comes high up, it may be mistaken for Secretiveness by the inexperienced observer. In like manner, Secretiveness and Acquisitiveness are sometimes confounded with Ideality: this happened in the case of Hare the murderer, in whose head the enemies of Phrenology ignorantly affirmed that Ideality was large, when the fact was exactly the reverse. These mistakes arise from the organs in question encroaching more than is usual upon the neighbouring ones; but an experienced investigator will never fall into them. Secretiveness, when large, gives a general breadth of head at the back part of the temple. Its tendency is to conceal. The following cut represents the organ large.

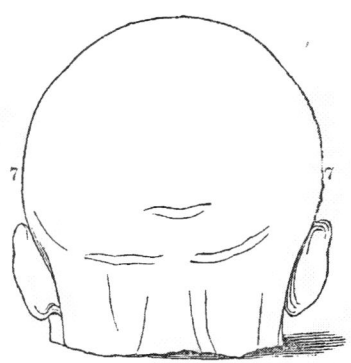

What is the character of a very secretive person?

He is reserved, and neither open nor explicit; is fond of stratagem and finesse, and delights in mystifying and deceiving. His pace is stealthy, his voice soft, his eyes sidelong, his eyelids half-closed, and he can hardly look an acquaintance in the face. A person with much Secretiveness is very fond of prying into the affairs of others, unless his mind be of a superior cast.

From what does cunning result?

From the excessive size and activity of this organ. Secretiveness, however, if well regulated by the moral sentiments, does not display itself in cunning, which is an abuse of the faculty.

Has it any thing to do in producing taciturnity?

It has. Taciturnity arises from Secretiveness and Cautiousness, accompanied, generally, with a small development of Language, and, in many cases, of Love of Approbation.

What good purpose is served by Secretiveness?

It communicates a power, often highly valuable, of hiding the manifestation of unpleasant feelings, which, without such restraint, would be sure to burst forth. It also gives us an insight into the feelings of others, and suspicion of their motives; hence secretive people are not easily imposed upon, and possess singular facility in detecting imposture, and seeing through plausibility and pretension. Secretiveness is of eminent use in war and diplomacy. Hannibal in the field, and Talleyrand and Fouché in the cabinet, sufficiently prove the truth of this remark. Secretiveness is the chief ingredient in what is called tact.

Is Secretiveness requisite for an actor?

No person can be a good performer without it. The actor must sink his own character in representing another; and this is chiefly effected by virtue of Secretiveness. Where Imitation exists, as it always does in good actors, the process is still more complete.

Is it an element in humour?

It enters very fully into what is called dry humour, such

as that of Dean Swift and Cervantes, where the writer, under the disguise of the most perfect simplicity and gravity, convulses us with laughter. Broad humour, such as that of Smollett and Rabelais, requires less of it, and into Irish humour it very sparingly enters.

In which sex is the feeling stronger?

In the female; and the size of the organ corresponds. A woman is obliged to conceal her feelings on a variety of occasions, where a man is placed under no such restraints. This is especially the case in reference to love matters. Let her attachment be ever so great, she dare not avow it till the man has made the fullest advances: she dare not even exhibit any sign of her feeling with regard to him, till he has given her ample reason to suppose that she is the object of his affection. In this, and various other displays of concealed emotion which the delicacy of the sex demands, we see the power of an active Secretiveness.[43]

What is the character of a person deficient in this faculty?

He is remarkable for candour and openness, speaks his mind freely, and is under little restraint. People of this kind ought never to be entrusted with a secret, as they feel a continual effort necessary to prevent them from divulging it.

Is the faculty active in any of the lower animals?

In many of them it is so, and their craft is generally, though not always, in proportion to the weakness or helplessness of the animal. The cunning of the fox and the cat is proverbial. Most birds are astute—witness the admirable manner in which the nests of many of them are hid from observation. The crocodile and turtle seem to show Secretiveness in the

---

[43] The hacknied but beautiful lines of Shakspeare are familiar to every one—

"She never told her love,
But let *concealment*, like a worm i' the bud,
Feed on her damask cheek."

skilful manner in which they hide their eggs in the sand, unless, indeed, we can suppose, that in so doing, they are guided by a particular blind instinct. Craft enables some animals to secure their prey, and others to avoid danger.

8. ACQUISITIVENESS.

State the position and nature of this organ.

It is situated at the anterior, inferior angle of the parietal bone, and the feeling connected with it gives the tendency to acquire and accumulate. When very powerful, there is an inordinate lust after riches. The person becomes a miser: the whole aim of his life is to hoard; and the loss of money he regards as the greatest of misfortunes. So strong is this feeling, that many persons, though wallowing in wealth, scarcely allow themselves the common necessaries of life. Such was the case with Elwes, who lived in great want and misery, although immensely rich—his fortune, at the time of his death, amounting to £700,000. Daniel Dancer, the miser, who left £60,000, slept for many years in an old sack, to save the expense of bedding, and never, even in the severest weather, allowed himself the luxury of a fire. He sustained life by begging, and literally died of starvation. The Duke of Marlborough, though worth £50,000 a year might be seen darning his stockings at the head of the army, and would walk home from the theatre on a rainy night to save sixpence.

What character results from large Acquisitiveness and deficient Conscientiousness?

The person will be thievishly inclined. If placed in unfavourable circumstances, it is hardly possible for him, with such an organization, to be otherwise than a thief.

If favourably situated, would he act the thief?

Possibly not. His pride, love of approbation, or terror of

discovery, might prevent him from stealing, but still at heart he would be a thief, and covet every thing he saw.

May a miser be a benevolent man ?

He may ; but he will show his benevolence in some other way than in giving money. Although he may exert himself vehemently, and spare no trouble to oblige a friend, it will be difficult or impossible to make him open his purse. It must be admitted, however, that the tendency of excessive Acquisitiveness is to "harden the heart, and petrify the feelings." Gold is the miser's divinity : he worships it as an idol, and extends his veneration to all who have a large share of it; hence wealthy people, however despicable their character, are apt to be held in profound respect by the acquisitive.

Are very acquisitive people usually happy ?

They are not. Having, in general, but one source of felicity, that of hoarding money, they are fretful and discontented, when their efforts at accumulation fall short of what they calculated upon: the loss of wealth annoys them exceedingly, and while they venerate, they, at the same time, envy those who are richer than themselves.

What is the result of small Acquisitiveness?

Indifference about making, and profusion in spending money. People of this description seldom talk about wealth; while with the acquisitive this is the favourite theme of conversation.

Does Acquisitiveness lead to the accumulation of money alone ?

No; it may show itself in accumulation of any kind. Some people are fond of hoarding books, medals, coins, curious shells, &c.: if a person has a liking for these things, and possesses large Acquisitiveness, he will naturally collect them, especially if this can be done at little expense.

Does this faculty display itself in early life?

When strong, it is manifested at a very early period. There are vast differences among children in this respect: one gives half of what he has to his playmate, another keeps all to himself: one school-boy will keep a halfpenny in his pocket a week before he has the heart to spend it; another gets quit of his little treasure almost as soon as it is in his possession.[44]

Does old age whet or diminish the activity of this organ?

It aggravates it to a great degree. A careful boy will make a miserly man. Avarice is commonly said to be the only passion which age does not blunt, but there is reason to doubt whether the vehemence of Destructiveness is mitigated by years. Old people frequently become exceedingly irascible and peevish, owing probably to the organ being stimulated by the discomforts and want of enjoyment so generally accompanying advanced life. Acquisitiveness and Destructivenes, therefore, may be held as increased, and not, like the other organs, diminished in activity by old age.[45]

Would you not infer that age blunts Acquisitiveness, seeing that theft is most common in early years?

Children steal more readily than grown people, because their caution and reflection are less. Adults see more

[44] The great Prince of Condé having occasion to go from home for some time, gave to his son, a young lad, eighty *louis d'or* for pocket money. On his return, the careful youth showed him the money, exclaiming "see, father, there is all the money you gave me, and I have not spent a single sous of it." The Prince was so disgusted with the penurious spirit of the lad, that he took the money and threw it into the street, telling the young miser that if he had not the manliness to spend it upon himself, he ought to have given it away.

[45] Why age should sharpen Acquisitiveness, while it blunts other faculties, it is difficult even to conjecture, but the fact is undeniable. A good story is told of an old Scotch nobleman, one of the Earls of Findlater, I believe, who, having found a farthing, and being solicited for the same by a beggar who saw him pick it up, put it carefully into his pocket, saying, "Na, na, puir body; find a farthing for yoursel."

clearly the consequences to which a discovery of theft would lead; and a man has naturally more respect for his reputation than a child. The desire of a man to possess any thing may be as strong as a child's; but to obtain it he will not readily adopt means which may involve him in disgrace. Independently of this, the moral feelings are actually weaker in childhood than at the subsequent periods of life.

May a thief possess benevolence?

Undoubtedly. He may rob you to-day and relieve you to-morrow with a liberal hand, if you are in distress. This fact may be easily verified by referring to the lives of famous pickpockets and highwaymen. George Barrington is a remarkable case in point. The celebrated outlaws, Robin Hood and Rob Roy, were instances in which a great deal of benevolent feeling co-existed with large Acquisitiveness and deficient Conscientiousness.[46] The generous behaviour of

---

[46] The passion for thieving, is in some individuals so intensely and irresistibly strong, as absolutely to amount to a disease. In such cases, it bears a very striking analogy to homicidal monomania. Victor Amadeus, King of Sardinia, had a strong passion for theft, and frequently indulged in the vice. The same was the case with Saurin, an intelligent and pious Swiss clergyman; and we frequently hear of ladies of rank and fortune stealing from the shops of haberdashers, while purchasing goods. The following remarkable case of thieving monomania, I extract from the London papers. Confirmed thieves seem all to labour under this affection:—

Central Criminal Court.—Henry Smith, a smart lad, aged thirteen, was convicted of stealing a diamond, the property of his father. The boy had been twice convicted, and kept solitary and whipped, but on his liberation he returned to his old habit of pilfering.

The little fellow, with tears, prayed the Court to send him to the convict ship to break him of thieving.

Court.—Why do you thieve?

Prisoner.—I cannot help it; I must do it.

The schoolmaster of Newgate was consulted as to the boy's intellect, and he was reported to be shrewd, of sound intellect, but so addicted to theft, that only last night he robbed a fellow-prisoner of a shilling. The Court complied with the prisoner's request.

the robber to Queen Margaret, after her defeat at Hexham, is matter of history; and many other instances of such men displaying great humanity might easily be recorded. In the prison of Copenhagen, for instance, Dr. Gall saw Pièrre Michel, a crafty and incorrigible thief, who stole for the sole purpose of giving away to the poor.

Is Acquisitiveness ever morbidly excited?

Such is sometimes the case. Irritation of the organ from an injury may force it into diseased activity, and thus make a thief of a person previously honest. Conscientious people, who become deranged, sometimes display a strong passion for stealing, on the same principle that individuals remarkable for chastity and purity of mind frequently indulge, during an attack of madness, in the most lascivious conversation. Dr. Gall mentions the cases of four women who, while pregnant, were strongly addicted to theft, and who yet exhibited no such inclination at other times. In such instances, the change of character which ensues can only be referred to diseased activity of the organ.

To what does the legitimate exercise of Acquisitiveness lead?

To a rational accumulation of wealth for proper purposes, as for the sake of securing comfort and independence to one's self and family. Carried much beyond this point, it is a contemptible vice, degrading to a human being.

Does the size of the organ differ in different nations?

Very much. It is said to be small in the Arragonese, and Castilians; and these people are not at all given to stealing. The Calmucs, who are notorious thieves, have a large development of the organ. It is generally large in Scotch, English, and Dutch heads; hence the vast fortunes acquired, and the high respect paid to wealth in Great Britain and Holland. It is small in the French head; a Frenchman is satisfied with a moderate competency, and when that is secured he generally retires from business to pass his life in pleasure; while the Briton and the Dutchman toil on till the last, in the accumulation of property. In France little respect is paid to a person merely on account of his wealth; while in some other countries, the mere whisper that a man is rich is sufficient to ensure him every homage and attention.

Is Acquisitiveness manifested by the lower animals?

Some of them exhibit its activity in great perfection. The magpie is a notorious thief, and carries its propensity so far as to steal what can be of no use to it. Cats are generally looked upon as thieves, and so are dogs; but I apprehend that it is not, as in the magpie, from an abstract principle of appropriation that they steal, but merely to gratify hunger. The industrious bee, in hoarding honey for its winter stores, shows the force of Acquisitiveness. The same remark applies to the beaver, which accumulates wood for the formation of its dwelling. The cow and the horse have the sense of property. Each goes to its own stall, and defends it against intrusion.

9. CONSTRUCTIVENESS.

Describe the position and function of this organ?

It is marked 9 in the bust, and lies in the temple, below and in front of Acquisitiveness. Its function may be described as the tendency to fashion or construct, and expertness in doing so. It is large in those who have a constructive or mechanical genius, such as Archimedes, Telford, Watt, Vauban, Michael Angelo, and Raphael. Dextrous artizans, and painters and sculptors who are eminent in the mechanical department of their avocations, must have the organ large; and accordingly we find that in them it is invariably above average. It is impossible to be even an expert tailor, carpenter, or milliner, without a good endowment of the organ. It alone, however, will not enable us to contrive an ingenious piece of machinery. Mechanical contrivers are not impelled by Constructiveness, but by intellect. The former, however, is absolutely necessary to embody, or realize, in a machine what the intellect suggests.

What follows when the organ is small?

The person is what we call clumsy-handed, and can do nothing with neatness and dexterity. Some men are so very remarkable in this respect that they cannot even make a pen, or shave themselves.

How does the faculty exhibit itself in the lower animals?

In various ways, and in some with exquisite nicety, witness the beautiful architecture of the honeycomb by that ingenious little artist the bee—the wonderful skill with which the beaver constructs its dwelling—and the art displayed by birds in the formation of their nests.

Is the force of this faculty in the lower animals in the ratio of their general intellect?

No more than in man. The most sagacious animals, such as the dog and elephant, never attempt a work of art, while creatures far inferior in general sagacity excel in such achievements. This is a decided proof that a special organ exists for the purpose of construction.

Do nations differ greatly with regard to the force of this organ?

Very much indeed. The head of the New Hollander is narrow in the region of Constructiveness, and his deficiency in this respect is notorious. The organ is largely developed in the Italian and French head, and more moderately in the English.

Can Constructiveness be abused?

Yes. The formation of engines for destroying human life, and the erection of such structures as the Sphinx, the Cretan Labyrinth, the Ear of Dionysius, and the Egyptian Pyramids, may all be regarded as abuses of the faculty. The same may be said of many of those trifling evanescent works of fancy, in which so much precious time is wasted by females in the middle and higher grades of society. Coining and fabricating forged notes are criminal abuses of the faculty.[50]

May a person void of constructive talent acquire it by diseased excitement of this organ?

Facts prove that this is possible. In such cases, however, the adventitious talent thus curiously acquired, will endure only so long as the excitement continues.

In what respect does the constructive talent of man differ from that of the lower animals?

The talent of the lower animals is specific and limited, The bee can construct only a honeycomb, the bird a nest, the beaver a dwelling of a particular form. No tuition can alter the dispositions of these creatures so as to make them build after any other fashion; whereas, the constructive talent of man is general in its operation; he works by a thousand different ways, and forms an infinity of distinct objects.

---

[50] There is a man in London who exhibits what he calls the learned fleas. He has contrived to employ those insects in a variety of occupations, such as drawing carriages and ships, carrying towers, and other pursuits equally momentous and important. Wonderful skill is displayed in the construction of the vehicles, &c. and in the admirable art with which the insects are attached to them—skill, which applied to proper purposes, might lead to great results, and do the artist honour. Such a childish application of great constructive talents, is surely an abuse of the faculty in question.

GENUS II.—SENTIMENTS.

What meaning is attached to the word Sentiment?

The term is applied to those affective faculties which, besides giving rise to inclinations, feel an emotion or affection which is not merely a propensity.

SPECIES. I.—INFERIOR SENTIMENTS.

10. SELF-ESTEEM.

How would you recognize a large Self-Esteem?

By the elevation which it gives to that part of the head immediately above Concentrativeness, and between it and the organ of Firmness. Both the organ and the physiognomical expression of the faculty are well represented in the subjoined engraving of a proud character.

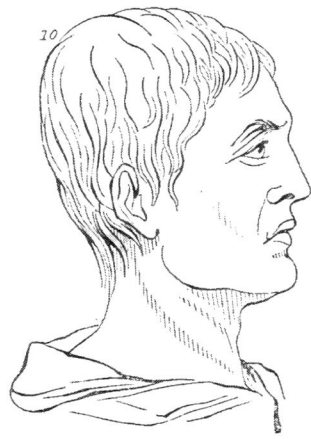

How was the organ discovered?

In the following manner:—Dr. Gall one day met with a weak-minded beggar, who had such an inordinate opinion of his own consequence, that he refused to work, considering labour to be entirely beneath his dignity. This man was the son of a rich merchant, and had been reduced to beggary by over-weening self-conceit preventing him from labouring for his bread. On examination, Dr. Gall observed a large prominence on the upper and back part of his head, which he supposed might be the seat of pride. Subsequent observations have fully verified his conjecture.

To what does excessive Self-Esteem lead?

To arrogance, to an immense opinion of one's self,[51] and, when accompanied by deficient Benevolence, to great selfishnesss.

What are the results of a small development?

Modesty and humility of demeanour. The person thinks little of himself, however admirable his merits, and is perfectly free from presumption. Such persons are great favourites with those who have much Self-Esteem. There is no collision of feeling between them—the humble mind unconsciously giving way to the proud one, and thus affording it gratification.

Is a great endowment of this faculty useful or the reverse?

Useful, rather than otherwise, if accompanied with good moral sentiments. It gives self-respect, a spirit of independence, and that proper pride which disdains every thing that is mean and dishonourable. Even bad men who have much Self-Esteem, are often prevented from acting improperly through the fear of compromising their dignity. A good

---

[51] It is the great Self-Esteem of the English which renders them so insufferable on the Continent—which leads them to decry all other nations, and to look upon themselves as in every respect the first people in the world. The songs which are addressed to the Self-Esteem of the nation, are universally popular: witness "Rule Britannia," and "Ye Mariners of England." That famous toast "The British Constitution—the pride of surrounding nations and the envy of the universe," is a preposterous ebullition of immoderate Self-Esteem. The Scotch Highlanders have a vast opinion of themselves, and I apprehend that the organ of Self-Esteem, is, generally speaking, decidedly larger in them than in their Lowland brethren.

endowment, by inspiring us with confidence in the soundness of our own opinions, is necessary to enable us to make head against popular errors and prejudices. Luther, in opposing the errors of the Church of Rome, was much indebted to this faculty. Had Dr. Gall been feebly gifted with it, and possessed, at the same time, predominating Love of Approbation, he never could have borne up against the torrent of ridicule and persecution which assailed him on account of his great discovery.

Is it possible to surmise the existence of large Self-Esteem without examining the head?

Yes. Those so endowed have generally an upright gait, carry their heads high, and have altogether an air of consequence about them. They are apt to speak in a pompous measured style, as if every word they uttered was highly oracular. They are great egotists, indulging largely in the use of the pronoun I,[52] and talking constantly of their own affairs. The pomposity of Self-Esteem is indeed highly imposing. Shallow men, by dint of it, often pass for being very profound; while others with ten times the talent but destitute of assumption, are frequently thought little of.

In which sex does the organ most predominate?

In the male. Men generally assume more than women,

---

[52] Take the following, from a work recently published, as a specimen:—
" Reader, when *I* was a child, it was not Gall, but some other galling phrenologist, who, seizing one of the protuberances of *my* reverend head, thank heaven it was not *my* nose, deliberately told *my* aunt Josephine, that the said bump contained the organ of matrimony. Now *my* aunt, not being deep in the science, as deliberately replied that she did not believe in any organ but the organ of music; whereat the good man, no way discouraged, immediately commenced feeling for the said organ. Indeed, sir, cried *I*, somewhat impatiently; indeed, sir, *I* have got no more bumps, and *I* should not have had that, only *I* fell down yesterday and knocked *my* head against the table. *My* aunt, Josephine, laughing aloud, the phrenologist was disconcerted, and *I*, glad of the opportunity, escaped from the room."—*Four Years' Residence in the West Indies, by F. W. N. Bayley.*

and their opinion of themselves is much greater. More men go deranged than women, from wounded pride.

What effect is produced by diseased excitement of this organ?

Its activity is enormously increased, and the person is apt to imagine himself a monarch, or even the Deity. In every madhouse lunatics of this description may be met with.

Mention a few of the forms in which Self-Esteem displays itself?

In a fondness for being placed in dignified situations, as on the magisterial bench, and an extreme sensibility to neglect or insult. "Better to reign in hell than serve in heaven," is the language of the faculty. Weak-minded people with much Self-Esteem, value themselves highly on account of their great connexions and acquaintances, if they happen to have any. Dr. Gall speaks of conceited individuals, who will not cut their nails lest it should appear that they are obliged to work. Many persons will not put their names upon their doors. This is the result of Self-Esteem. They imagine themselves to be people of such consequence that all the world should know where they reside. Those with a very strong endowment of this faculty, are fond of taking the lead on all occasions, and are apt to be disobedient to superiors. Leaders of mutinies have the organ well marked. Great Self-Esteem, especially if combined with deficient Conscientiousness and a mean intellect, induces people to speak uncharitably and harshly of those whose religious sentiments differ from their own. They look upon their own particular creed as the only one which can possibly be true; and, if Destructiveness is largely developed, do not scruple to consign all other sects to eternal punishment in the life to come. Persons of this stamp will frequently not associate with those who think differently in religious matters from themselves. " Get behind me, sinner;

thou art less righteous than I." Such is the motto of these modern Pharisees.

Does Self-Esteem produce vanity?

No. The proud man despises the opinions of others; the vain man lives, as it were, upon them. "The man is too proud to be vain," was a remark of Dean Swift, and is founded on a correct view of human nature.[53]

Why are many of those who figure as great patriots and defenders of popular rights thorough tyrants at heart?

This seems to arise from those pseudo-patriots possessing a great endowment of Self-Esteem, with deficient Benevolence and Conscientiousness. The first makes them impatient of seeing others placed in higher stations than themselves, and the deficiency of the two last renders them unscrupulous in their usage of others. To pull down those who sit in high places, they make tools of the populace, whom probably they dislike a great deal more than do those whose overthrow they are meditating. Knaves of this description frequently get into Parliament, and other public situations, by impudent pretensions to superior patriotism.[54]

---

[53] "The proud man is penetrated with a sense of his superior merit, and from the height of his grandeur, treats with contempt or indifference all other mortals; the vain man attaches the utmost importance to the judgment of others, and ardently seeks for their approbation. The proud man expects that the world should come and discover his merit; the vain man strikes at every door to draw attention towards him, and supplicates even the smallest portion of honour. The proud man despises the marks of distinction which constitute the happiness of the vain one. The proud man is disgusted by indiscreet eulogiums; the vain man inhales incense with rapture, however unskilfully scattered upon him; the proud man, even under the most imperious necessity, never descends from his elevation; the vain man humbles himself even to the ground, provided by this means he attain his end."—*Gall, Sur Les Fonctions du Cerveau*, tome iv. p. 296. This discriminative sketch is worthy of Theophrastus.

[54] "Ces hommes renverseroient tous les trones pour s'eriger euxmêmes en despotes. Ainsi l'organization confirme ce que l'histoire de tous les temps nous a enseigné sur le but des révolutions: *otez-vous de la que je m'y mette.*"—*Gall.*

Do any of the inferior animals possess the faculty of Self-Esteem?

The turkey, the peacock, and the horse are conceived to do so. Napoleon's favourite steed seems to have had the feeling strong: when ridden by any other than his Imperial Master, he appeared depressed, and to feel as if degraded; but so soon as the Emperor mounted him, he raised his head erect, looking inflated with pride, as if conscious that he had the honour of carrying one who was greater than all others. The animal's sagacity was here equal to his pride, as he must have caught the idea of his master's rank by remarking the respectful manner in which he was universally treated. The dislike which one dog has to see another caressed, arises from wounded Self-Esteem.

11. LOVE OF APPROBATION.

Describe the position and function of this organ.

It lies on each side of the organ of Self-Esteem. The objects sought for by the faculty are, esteem and admiration, and it is gratified by praise. It also prompts us to set an excessive value upon the opinions of the particular circle in which we move, however absurd or pernicious those may be. When very strong, there is a constant and fidgetty desire to please and be admired by every body, a morbid appetite for praise, and a longing to know what the world thinks of us. The person so endowed dresses well, or employs other means to excite admiration. His leading aim is to procure applause; he lives upon incense, and is wretched if he does not obtain it. In short, as pride is the abuse of Self-Esteem, so is vanity that of Love of Approbation. Combined, they produce ambition. This organ is very large in the busts of Themistocles, who from his earliest years displayed an unquenchable love of glory, and often declared that the victories of Miltiades would not allow him to sleep.[55] The feeling seems to have been very strong in Alexander the Great, Napoleon, and Charles XII. of Sweden.

Have not women more vanity than men?

Such is generally the case, although some men have the passion in great excess. Women are easily flattered, and soon become partial to those who bestow upon them this species of adulation. Women frequently go deranged from diseased Love of Approbation, which is seldom the case with the other sex.

What is the demeanour of a person with a great endowment of this faculty?

It is conciliating, courteous, and polite, very different from the hard austerity and pomp of Self-Esteem. Beaux, masters of ceremonies, teachers of dancing, bowing silk mercers, &c., afford good illustrations of the natural language of the faculty.

Does the feeling display itself in any other way?

Yes: when combined with deficient Conscientiousness, it disposes the person to "shoot with the long bow," and to be addicted to boasting. If he is naturally a coward, his Love of Approbation will dispose him to talk largely of valiant feats performed by himself—all for the purpose of disguising

---

[55] Themistocles was not a strictly conscientious man, as is proved by his treatment of Aristides, and his proposal to destroy the ships of the other Greek powers for the purpose of giving his native country the supremacy, at a time when these powers were at peace with it, and had no reason to fear such an outrage. When, however, the King of Persia came to claim his promise that he would lead the barbarian forces against Greece, his Love of Approbation seems to have taken alarm, and rather than do a deed which must have blasted his reputation for ever among his countrymen, he chose, although the Athenians had used him most shamefully, and well deserved punishment, to die by his own hands. It is not probable that Conscientiousness had much influence in stopping him, and far less fear. The feeling by which he was arrested in his career of vengeance was, in all probability, Love of Approbation.

his conscious pusillanimity. Men, for the most part, wish to make it appear that they possess those good qualities in which they are deficient; hence the coward, like the ass in the lion's skin, tries to assume the guise of valour.

By whom is Love of Approbation most displayed?

By those whose success in their profession depends upon public applause, such as actors, painters, &c.: it is in the gratification of this feeling, indeed, that the chief reward of their exertions often consists. People who are fond of appearing much before the public, either in the shape of orators, lecturers, chairmen of meetings, movers of addresses, or any other in which they will be spoken of, and their sayings and doings blazoned in the newspapers, have generally a large organ of Love of Approbation.[56]

Does vanity manifest itself the same way with every one?

No. The way in which it manifests itself depends upon the other faculties. A vain man with a good endowment of Tune, and a small organ of Number, will be vain of his musical genius, and comparatively indifferent to praise on account of his powers of calculation. Swindlers, pickpockets, robbers, and even murderers often boast of their feats. If a man excels in any thing, and possesses much Love of Approbation, he will be apt to boast of his eminence in that particular walk; hence we have men who are vain of their powers of eating and drinking. The vain man always wishes to be esteemed eminent in his profession, whether it

---

[56] "I love vanity" observes, Dr. Gall "because it gives rise to a thousand artificial wants, augments the comforts of life, embellishes our habitations, and employs and gives support to the industrious. It is to it, in a great degree, that we are indebted for the flourishing state of the arts and sciences. Collections of sculpture, of paintings, of natural history, of books—our gardens, our monuments, our palaces, would be either paltry or altogether awanting, without the inspiration of vanity, the love of distinction."

be that of poet, statesman, physician, divine, pickpocket, glutton, drunkard, or bravo.[57]

Do the lower animals display this faculty?

Some do. Dogs are exceedingly fond of caresses and approbation. I remember of a favourite terrier bringing a rat which he had killed to my bed-room door, and scraping for admittance, evidently that I might see the good service he had done. The animal had been trained to rat-killing, and evidently knew that in slaying one of these creatures he had done an action which would be applauded. The violent efforts of the race-hose in the struggle for victory evidently proceed from Love of Approbation. The faculty is active in the monkey, which is fond of gaudy dresses.

What follows when the organ is very small?

A marked indifference to praise and to the opinions of the world. It is unfortunate when a person is so circumstanced, for the love of being well thought of is certainly one of the great incentives to the performance of generous deeds.

Does good ever result from excessive vanity?

Sometimes to the public—rarely to the individual. For instance, men, from a love of ostentation, often put down their names as donors to public charities, to which, otherwise, they would not have contributed a farthing. The magnificent sepulchral monuments of "Père la Chaise" are erected, in a great measure, at the instigation of vanity on the part of the families of the deceased. The same feeling has much to do in the erection and endowment of hospitals to which wealthy individuals, such as Guy and Heriot, appropriate their fortunes.

---

[57] "A large organ of Love of Approbation, in a head of great general size, gives origin to the ambition of a Bonaparte; while a large development of the organ in a small head produces frivolous vanity, like that of the Hindoos, whose heads, as Lady Irwin says, 'are toyshops filled with trifling wares.'"—*Phrenological Journal*, vol. viii. p. 641.

Can a person be amiable without Love of Approbation?

Not easily. This feeling enters strongly into the composition of an amiable character. It gives the desire to please and the fear to offend, which, in every situation of life are so desirable.[58]

12. CAUTIOUSNESS.

What is the tendency of this organ?

To produce a feeling of circumspection, and when very active, fear. Those in whom it predominates are never rash: they are what is called "prudent characters," who seldom get into scrapes, and scrupulously weigh the consequences of every word and action.

Does great Cautiousness necessarily lead to cowardice?

Not unless it greatly predominates over Combativeness. Some of the greatest heroes were distinguished for circumspection: such was the case with Hannibal, Fabius, and many others. The skull of Bruce shows a large organ of Cautiousness, and this feeling was a marked one in his character.

---

[58] The activity of this feeling is at present a great bar to the progress of Phrenology, but, by and by, it will assist in disseminating the science. People with much Love of Approbation are exceedingly shy of doing any thing which the public mind deems unfashionable; they go with the majority, no matter whether that be right or wrong. At present the number of persons who understand, and believe in Phrenology is less than of those who are ignorant of, and do not believe in it. This difference is gradually diminishing; and as soon as a nearer approximation is made between the strength of the two parties; as soon as it appears perfectly manifest that the doctrines are every where gaining ground, and becoming *fashionable* and *popular*, then will the ranks of those who avow faith in them be increased by hosts of such individuals rushing breathlessly in to tender their adherence at the eleventh hour. The opinions of these fair weather converts, not being based upon that rational conviction resulting from knowledge, are of little consequence as testifying to the truth of the science; but as regards the general interests of Phrenology, they are valuable, in so far as so many obstacles to its diffusion are removed, and greater opportunities afforded of practically applying its principles than exist at the present moment.

CAUTIOUSNESS. 87

Is a large organ of Cautiousness easily discriminated?

More so, perhaps, than any other. It gives a rounded and bulging fulness to the middle of the parietal bones, under which it is situated.

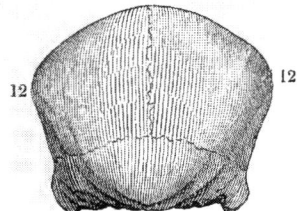
Large Cautiousness.

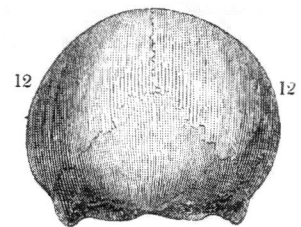
Small Cautiousness.

The first of the above engravings represents the skull of a timorous, faint-hearted female: the second that of General Wurmser, a man remarkable for the recklessness of his courage.

Is this organ well established?

It is one of the best authenticated of the whole series. Those in whom it is large, have uniformly the feeling of circumspection strongly stamped upon their character.

What is the consequence of a small development?

Rashness. The person is extremely imprudent; he speaks and acts without thinking; and, if engaged in business, it is ten to one that he ruins himself.

What most powerfully excites the organ?

Sudden and imminent danger. Soldiers in battle are sometimes panic-struck, and take to flight from the violent excitement of Cautiousness. Before a battle, it is more likely to be active than when the other faculties are fairly called into play by the heat of the contest.

What good purpose is served by this faculty?

It keeps people out of mischief, and renders them prudent. A community in which the feeling did not exist, would soon go to destruction.

Is the organ ever diseased?

It sometimes is; and the person becomes straightway the victim of the most miserable apprehensions. I have remarked that this organ is uniformly large in those afflicted with hypochondria, which, indeed, is a morbid affection of the organ.[59]

Is the organ larger in the female than in the male?

It is so, not only in the human species, but also in the inferior animals.

Is the feeling very strong in any of the lower animals?

In some, exceedingly so: the sheep and mouse, for example, are remarkably timid. Animals which prowl by night, such as the owl and the cat, show the manifestations of active Cautiousness. Some of the monkey tribe, when they go on a plundering expedition, place sentries to warn them of danger. The chamois, the wild goose, the crane, the starling, and the buzzard are remarkable for circumspection, and act like the monkies in appointing sentinels. In all these animals that portion of the head, corresponding to the seat of the organ of Cautiousness in the human subject, is much developed.

Does the size of the organ vary much in different nations?

It varies considerably. In the French head it is rather small, which partly accounts for the recklessness of the national character, and the state of disturbance in which that

---

[59] By many authors hypochondria is regarded as a disease of the digestive viscera; but that its real seat is the organ of Cautiousness, has been amply demonstrated by Dr. Andrew Combe, in the Phrenological Journal, vol. iii. p. 51.

BENEVOLENCE. 89

singular people keep not only themselves, but all Europe. In the English, Scotch, and German head, the organ is large, and smaller in the Irish. Scotch prudence and Irish thoughtlessness have long been proverbial. It is very large in the Hindoo and Peruvian head, and accounts for the great timidity of character displayed by these nations, its influence not being modified by the counteracting influence of Combativeness.[60]

SPECIES II.—SUPERIOR SENTIMENTS.

13. BENEVOLENCE.

Where does this organ lie?

Immediately before the fontanel (or opening of the head, as it is vulgarly called),[61] in the upper and middle part of the frontal bone; and it extends downward to the top of the forehead. It is known by the elevation which, when large, it gives to the middle of the anterior region of the top of the head.[62]

---

[60] It is observed that when this organ is large, there is also very generally an ample development of Cautiousness; and between the functions of the two organs a considerable affinity undoubtedly exists.

[61] The fontanel is at the meeting of the coronal and sagittal sutures. In the young child it is cartilaginous. From the time of birth it begins to contract, and is generally completely ossified and closed between the second and third year.

[62] In paintings of the head of Christ, the organs of Benevolence and Veneration are represented as greatly developed, while the posterior region where the propensities reside, is made exceedingly small. Is this generally received likeness of Jesus purely ideal? If so, it shows that the form of head which painters have considered appropriate to an eminently amiable and virtuous character, is precisely the same as that assigned to such charac-

Was a high forehead, before the time of Gall, supposed to indicate benevolence of disposition?

There is reason to believe so. Shakspeare speaks of "foreheads villanous low;" and the ancients, in designing their deities generally invested them with broad and lofty foreheads, thus indicating commanding intellect, and distinguished benevolence. The subject, however, was not philosophically thought of till Gall took it up, and demonstrated that the sentiment depends upon a special organ of the brain.

What effect on the character is produced by a large organ?

The individual is distinguished by the kindness and mercy of his disposition. He is generous in his sentiments, averse to give pain and uneasiness, charitable, and inclined to think well of every body, and do good to all his fellow-creatures. Some of the ancient philosophers, such as Plato and Socrates, are splendid instances of the beauty and power of this noble sentiment. The story of the good Samaritan is a fine specimen of benevolent feeling. One of the grandest instances on record occurs in the history of Sir Philip Sidney, who, when mortally wounded at the battle of Zutphen, and suffering under the tortures of excessive thirst, presented the water, which he was in the

---

ters by phrenologists. Dr. Gall, however, is of opinion, that the above representation is not imaginary, but conveys a genuine likeness of the great original. "It is at least probable," says he, "that the general type of the form of Christ's head has been handed down to us. Saint Luke was a painter, and in that capacity, is it not likely that he would wish to preserve the features of his Master? It is certain that this likeness of the Saviour's head is of high antiquity: we find it in the most ancient mosaics and paintings. In the second century, the Gnostics possessed images both of Christ and Saint Paul. Hence neither Raphael, nor any painter of more ancient date, invented the admirable configuration of head which has been assigned to Jesus."

act of raising to his mouth, to a dying soldier whom he saw eagerly eyeing it—saying "take that; your want is even greater than mine."[63] In Christ's sermon on the Mount we have a sublime emanation of blended Benevolence and Conscientiousness. Indeed, throughout the whole of the New Testament the supremacy of the moral sentiments shines forth with a lustre not to be equalled in any other code of religion or morality.

What happens when the organ is very small?

The person is careless of the welfare of others, disobliging and selfish. Unless he has some end to serve, it will be impossible for him to do a kindly action. Such a man can never be a true and disinterested friend. Moloch, as represented in "Paradise Lost," is an instance of a total destitution of this faculty; and nearly the same may be said of Ahab and Jezebel in the book of Kings, of Shakspeare's Iago, Moore's Zeluco, and also of Varney, in the romance of "Kennilworth." The organ, according to Dr. Gall, was very deficient in the head of Robespièrre. Some of the Roman Emperors, as Domitian, Commodus, Caligula, Heliogabolus, and Nero, seem to have been as nearly void of the sentiment as we can suppose creatures not absolutely denizens of Pandemonium, to be. The busts of these men

---

[63] " Man," observes Gall, " is generally more good, kind-hearted, and just, than he is wicked and unjust. People of simple manners—the comfortable peasant, the industrious artizan, for example, are very benevolent towards their equals. We rarely see among them an orphan who fails to meet with the assistance which his situation demands. They often treat them as they would their own children, and not unfrequently with even greater kindness. Seldom do the poor, who knock at their doors, return empty-handed: their direct impulse is always one of kindness towards the unfortunate." Gall himself had a large organ of Benevolence, and, in harmony with this development, was inclined to view human nature with a generous eye. Those in whom the organ is small have, from their own consciousness, a tendency to think meanly of their fellow-creatures, and to form a low estimate of human virtue.

represent a poor development of Benevolence with a predominating basilar region. Take as an example the subjoined representation of Nero's head.

May Benevolence co-exist with great roughness of manner?

Nothing is more common; but the general tendency of the feeling is to communicate sweetness to the disposition, and to soften the manners. Some people are absolutely ashamed of the Benevolence they possess, and try to hide it under a rough exterior: "rough diamonds" of this description are occasionally to be met with. Dr. Johnson was an instance of distinguished Benevolence combined with coarseness of manners—the *fortiter in modo* with the *suaviter in re.*

What are the abuses of Benevolence?

The tendency to yield to every kind of solicitation is one; whence the individual becomes the prey of mendicants and impostors: he impoverishes himself to do good to others, and has his brain constantly filled with Utopian schemes of philanthropy.[64]

Have the lower animals this organ?

They have, to some extent. In them it shows itself chiefly by tractability and gentleness. A good tempered dog or horse can be known by the shape of the head. The

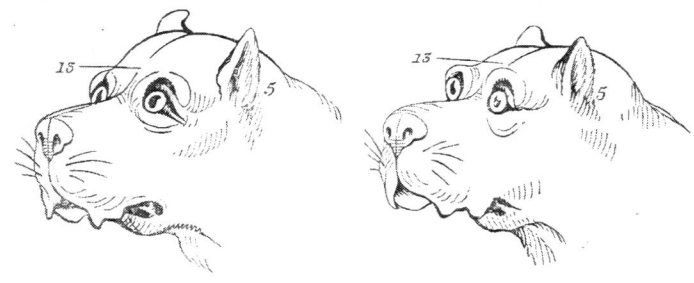

13 Benevolence large. 13 Benevolence small.
5 Combativeness small. 5 Combativeness large.

celebrated race horse " Flying Childers," had a very low and flat forehead, and his temper was extremely vicious. In the spaniel and Newfoundland dog, both distinguished for goodness of temper, the organ is much larger than in the bull-dog, whose dispositions are naturally morose and savage. The roebuck, which is a mild-tempered animal, has a prominence, and the chamois, which is the reverse, a depression over the region of Benevolence.

---

[64] I know several individuals in this situation, and in the whole of them there is great height of forehead—in other words, a large development of the organ of Benevolence. The fanciful impracticabilities of Mr. Owen seem to result from the immoderate action of this organ, combined with that of Hope in excess.

14. VENERATION.

What is the nature of the faculty connected with this organ?

It may be described as that feeling which produces veneration in general, or respect for those whom we consider worthy of reverence. When directed to the Supreme Being, it gives the tendency to religious adoration. Some persons object to there being an organ in the brain which gives the tendency to religious feeling, on the ground that such an idea is hostile to the doctrine of a revelation; but this, as Spurzheim remarks, is an unfounded objection—religion of one kind or another having existed long before the dates of the Old and New Testaments, in which the Christian revelation is handed down to us. The emotion communicated by this organ is, in itself, blind, and gives no insight into the truth or falsehood of a religion. The soundness or unsoundness of any creed is tested by another set of faculties, viz. the Intellectual, and cannot be taken cognizance of by a mere sentiment which simply feels, and is incapable of reasoning. In reference to the present faculty, Mr. Combe finely observes that " as Nature has implanted the organs of Veneration and Wonder in the brain, and the corresponding sentiments in the mind, it is a groundless terror to apprehend that religion can ever be extinguished, or even endangered, by the arguments or ridicule of the profane. Forms of worship may change, and particular religious tenets may now be fashionable and subsequently fall into decay; but while the human heart continues to beat, awe and veneration for the Divine Being will ever animate the soul: the worshipper will cease to kneel, and the hymn of adoration to rise, only when the race of man becomes extinct."

Where is the organ situated?

Immediately behind that of Benevolence, and directly over the fontanel. It occupies the middle of the top of the head. The annexed engraving of the head of St. Bruno displays a great development of the organ. Benevolence is also very large. Such a configuration of brain is highly favourable to religion and virtue. Men so constituted are a law unto themselves. They revere their Maker, and have an instinctive tendency to love and treat with tenderness the whole human race.

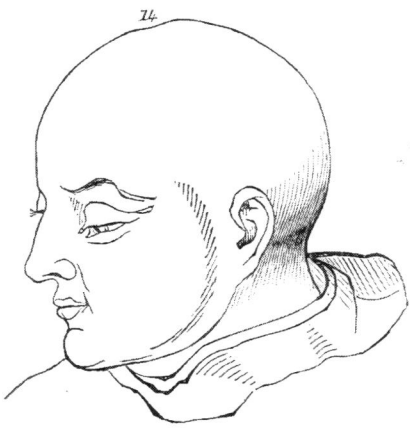

This organ was large in the head of Voltaire: why then was he an infidel?

Because he was not convinced of the divine origin of Christianity. No man can venerate what he does not conceive to be true. Voltaire, however, venerated the Deity, of whose existence he entertained no doubt.[66] The respect

---

[66] See " Observations on some Objections to Phrenology, founded on a part of the Cerebral Development of Voltaire," by Mr. Simpson.—*Phrenological Journal*, vol. iii. p. 564.

which this writer showed for princes, and the gratification he experienced in associating with them arose undoubtedly from his large Veneration.

May a person believe in a particular religion, and yet have little Veneration?

Undoubtedly. Belief may be a matter of pure reason, though, in general, the judgment is swayed by the feelings. The merely intellectual believer, however, will never be a very ardent disciple of that religion in which his faith is placed. He may believe in a Great First Cause without inclining to adore.

Under what other forms does the faculty display itself?

In a respect for rank, for existing institutions, for antiquity, and for the ruling powers. It is the grand natural maintainer of subordination of the lower ranks to the higher, and of the submission of children to parents and teachers. A person with this sentiment strong, is overawed in coming into the presence of those whose rank or other valued distinction, is greatly superior to his own.[67] Such persons, if their intellect is not of that respectable order which disposes them to appreciate intellectual characters, will be more flattered by the acquaintanceship of a silly lord than by that of such a man as Locke or Newton.

[67] "The faculty may be manifested in reverence for Jupiter, or the Lama of Thibet, or graven images, or the God of the universe; for crocodiles, cats, or the Great Mogul, or Catholic priests, or Presbyterian ministers, or rusty coins, or a titled aristocracy, or the ornaments and furniture of a church. To those who have it disproportionately strong, the word 'old' is synonymous with 'venerable;' and in their view, no institution or doctrine, however hurtful and absurd, is, if sanctioned by antiquity, to be at all meddled with. They obstinately adhere to the religious tenets instilled into them in childhood, and will not listen to arguments tending to support doctrines of a different kind. When, on the other hand, the organ of Veneration is moderate, and the intellect is acute and enlightened, the individual, unwarped by prejudice and feeling, regards only the intrinsic merits of the doctrines and institutions which prevail around him, and shapes his opinions accordingly."—*Phrenological Journal*, vol. viii. p. 598.

VENERATION.

Whence arises the love for collecting antiques?

From Veneration combined with Acquisitiveness. The first disposes us to value the object on account of its antiquity; the second makes us long to possess it. People with small Veneration have little abstract love for any thing, merely because it is ancient.

Does Veneration display itself in the same way with every one?

No; it is directed very much by the other faculties. A man of high intellect and Veneration will venerate intellectual characters; another, with Veneration and Combativeness, great warriors; and a third, with Veneration and Acquisitiveness, will venerate the rich. The two former, on beholding the cross, the hunting horn, or the bones of Charlemagne, in the church at Aix-la-Chapelle, will feel deep awe at the sight of these relics of so renowned a statesman and hero; the third, having no sympathy with valour and genius, will gaze upon them unmoved, while he would look with sensations of great respect, and even awe, upon such a man as Mr. Rothschild. It is to be observed, however, that a powerful and cultivated understanding tends to keep Veneration within rational bounds.

When the organ is strongly excited, in what manner does it affect the character?

In producing keen religious or devotional feelings, terminating sometimes even in madness.

How happens it that irreligious people sometimes become, all of a sudden, very devout?[68]

This proceeds from sudden excitement of the organs of Veneration and Wonder. The individual has, probably,

---

[68] It also oftentimes happens that, in cases of serious illness, people become very religious, who, for many years previous, exhibited no devotional feeling. This, I believe, may often be accounted for, on the well known principle of cerebral excitement reviving lost ideas. The brain is stimu-

been exposed to circumstances which call them into activity, as the declamation of some enthusiastic preacher, and the result is a vehement fit of religion, which continues so long as the stimulus operates on the brain.

A person then may become religious whether his organ of Veneration be large or small, seeing that a small organ may be stimulated as well as a large one?

It is only the predominating organs that are very likely to be excited; a small organ is by no means equally liable to be acted upon in this manner, and when really stimulated, does not give rise to the same intensity of feeling. If it were so acted upon, the person would be religious compared to what he formerly was, but still his feelings on this point would be far inferior in energy to those of another person, with a larger organ of Veneration in the same state of excitement.[69]

May a person have a great deal of religious feeling and yet not be virtuous?

Undoubtedly: witness the instances of Louis XI. of France, Philip II. of Spain, Catherine de' Medici, and the "Bloody" Queen Mary, all of them religious devotees, and yet most

---

lated by the disease, and the religious impressions instilled into us in childhood are brought back to cheer the sufferer on the bed of sickness, and smooth his path to the grave. Various instances of the resuscitative power of excited brain are given in this work.

69 An acquaintance with Phrenology must be of great use in preventing people from running into fanaticism, and in allaying religious melancholy. If a man knows that such violent states of feeling arise from excitement existing in his brain, he will set about counteracting them; whereas, when he is ignorant of this fact, he will be apt to mistake the impression under which he labours for the effect of some supernatural cause; and the illusion, instead of being checked, will probably go on increasing, till it terminates in madness. An eminent phrenologist informs me, that he is acquainted with several ladies who have actually been reclaimed from fanaticism by studying Phrenology. I believe the statement, and can easily imagine that a knowledge of this science will go far to check the accession of most forms of lunacy.

worthless characters. If the precepts, however, which a religion inculcates are, in themselves, of a strictly moral character, the respect for their authority inspired by this sentiment, will naturally tend to make people more virtuous. The precepts of Christianity are of this kind, and when strictly followed, can only lead to sound morality: those of some other forms of religion being depraved, conduce to vice. The Hindoo who throws his child beneath the wheels of the car of Juggernaut, acts as much under the influence of Veneration, as the enlightened Christian who worships the true God. The difference consists in this, that in the one case it is a misdirected impulse, in the other, it is an impulse guided by reason.

In which sex is the feeling of Veneration more energetic?

In the female. Women are more susceptible of religious impressions than men, and are generally the first to be caught by new doctrines. They have also a greater tendency to respect rank, and are naturally aristocratic in their ideas. Few women are enamoured of republican principles.[70] Self-Esteem being weaker and Veneration stronger in

---

[70] Some years ago, religious monomania was exceedingly common in the West of Scotland, among a class of people who went by the name of Rowites. These fanatics were mostly young females, in the middle and upper classes of society; and the extent to which they carried their insane ravings was most astounding. An enthusiastic young woman was the High Priestess of this sect: her they supposed to be divinely commissioned, and even gifted with the power of working miracles. At length she left the place, and the excitement of her presence being withdrawn, the mania subsided. I agree with Dr. Mackintosh in thinking, that a few weeks' work on the tread-mill, with scanty fare, would have cured of their fantasies the over-fed and idle young ladies who indulged in this egregious folly. The reader will find in the ninth volume of the Phrenological Journal a series of acute and instructive papers on this kind of insanity, entitled "Observations on Religious Fanaticism: illustrated in a comparison of the belief and conduct of noted religious enthusiasts with those of patients in the Montrose Lunatic Asylum." By W. A. Browne, Esq., the superintendent of that institution.

women than in men, nature has obviously intended that this sex should be led by, and obey, the other.

What were the circumstances which lighted up the fires of Smithfield, and prompted the massacre of St. Bartholomew?

These horrible immolations of innocent persons at the shrine of bigotry, seem to have resulted from a violent excitement of this organ, combined with great Destructiveness and Self-Esteem, and a lamentable lack of Benevolence and knowledge. A weak or uninformed intellect, acting under the inspiration of excited religious feeling, would make the perpetrators imagine they were doing a deed highly acceptable to the Deity; and Destructiveness coming into play, and not being counteracted by Benevolence, would urge them on fiercely to the commission of these diabolical atrocities.

15. FIRMNESS.

Where is this organ situated?

Behind that of Veneration, on the summit of the head, to which, when very large, it gives a towering appearance.

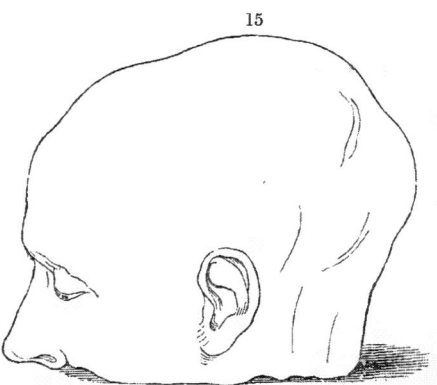

What is the nature of its faculty?

The name sufficiently designates this. When it is very

large, the individual is distinguished for great perseverance. Whatever he undertakes, whether for good or evil, he pursues steadily; and the general cast of his mind is firm and decided. He encounters misfortunes heroically, and endures physical pain with unshrinking stoicism. He is not to be turned from his purposes, but is rather apt to be unyielding and obstinate. There are great differences in people as to their capability of resisting solicitation. This, other things being equal, arises from the different degrees in which they are endowed with Firmness. The faculty tends to keep the other powers of the mind in a state of continuous action, enabling those higly gifted with it to pursue steadily the natural bent of their talents. Where the development is small, the person is fickle and infirm of purpose. He may possess excellent abilities, but from want of perseverance they are not properly cultivated and brought out. Instability and indecision of character are uniformly accompanied with a deficient size of the organ: and these qualities appear still more prominent where, along with such deficiency, there is a large development of Cautiousness.

What is obstinacy?

Obstinacy is an abuse of Firmness, and the result of a great development of this organ, with small or moderate Conscientiousness. A strictly honest man can never be long or wilfully obstinate, however great his Firmness: the latter always gives way before what he conceives to be the dictates of justice.

Is it possible to have too much Firmness?

When the dispositions are naturally virtuous, and the intellect good, this is impossible, as the faculty in question only leads them more strongly and perseveringly in their natural current. When, however, there is a predominance of vice in the character, great Firmness may act perniciously, by causing an obstinate perseverance in evil.

In what characters would you expect to find the organ large?

In those who show unshaken constancy and indomitable perseverance. It must have been large in Luther and Knox. King Robert Bruce's skull shows a great development of it; and he evinced the feeling to a wonderful degree. It is large in those who manifest great determination in crime, as Haggart; and also in those whose steadiness of friendship nothing can shake. The firmness of Captains Ross and Parry is well known, and the organ is very ample in the heads of those eminent navigators. I am told that it is remarkably large in General Jackson, the American President, a man whose firmness of purpose borders on obstinacy. The North American Indians are remarkable for their unconquerable fortitude, and the dogged indifference with which they submit to the most horrible tortures: in them it is greatly developed. It must have been very large in Marshal Ney, who possessed astonishing firmness of character.

16. CONSCIENTIOUSNESS.

In what manner does the faculty connected with this organ display itself?

In inducing sentiments of strict justice.[71] He in whom it is strongly manifested is a person of stern integrity: he pays his debts, does what he considers his duty, and is incapable of dissimulation or falsehood—adhering, in its strictest sense, to the noble maxim of doing unto others as he would be done by. Such a man will rather die of starvation than steal—

---

[71] "The laws of honour, as apprehended by some minds, are founded on the absence of Conscientiousness, with great predominance of Self-Esteem and Love of Approbation. If a gentleman is conscious that he has unjustly given offence to another, it is conceived by many that he will degrade himself by making an apology; that it is his duty to fight, but not to acknow-

rather go to the block than violate the dictates of his conscience. If he commits a wrong he is the first to acknowledge it, and feels uneasy till he makes ample reparation. He has, in short, a vivid and peculiar pleasure in acting honestly.

Where is the organ situated?

At each side of Firmness.

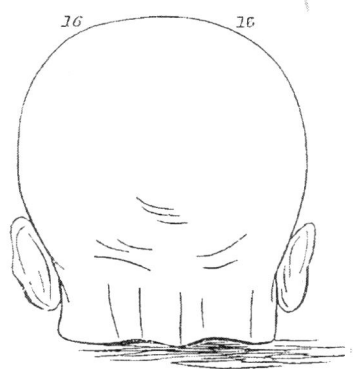

Large Conscientiousness.

What follows when the organ is small?

Lying, theft, hypocrisy, evil-speaking, dissimulation, and general want of principle are apt to be the consequences of

---

ledge himself in fault. This is the feeling produced by powerful Self-Esteem and Love of Approbation, with great deficiency of Conscientiousness. Self-Esteem is mortified by an admission of fallibility, while Love of Approbation suffers under the feeling that the esteem of the world will be lost by such an acknowledgment; and if no higher sentiment be present in a sufficient degree, the wretched victim will go to the field and die in support of conduct that is indefensible. When Conscientiousness is strong, the possessor feels it no degradation to acknowledge himself in fault, when he is aware that he is wrong: in fact, he rises in his own esteem by doing so, and knows that he acquires the respect of the world; while, if fully conscious of being in the right, there is none more inflexible than he."—*Combe's System of Phrenology, 4th edition,* vol. i., p. 358.

CONSCIENTIOUSNESS.

such an unfortunate configuration, the propensities being left in a great measure unbridled.

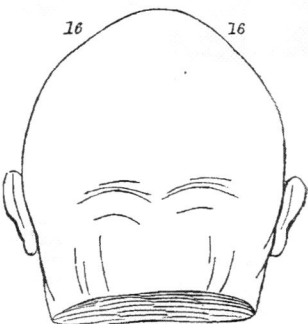

Small Conscientiousness.

May a deficiency of the sentiment display itself otherwise than in the commission of what society would deem crimes?

Yes. The not keeping appointments and promises, the telling of "white lies," jilting, coquetry, quibbling, professional quackery and humbug, writing impertinent anonymous letters, puffing trashy works, giving false characters to servants, borrowing books and umbrellas and not returning them, taking possession of another man's seat in the theatre or coach, knowing that you have no right to do so, and that it will put him to inconvenience, are all breaches of honesty, and indicate a small or moderate development of the organ. Divulging secrets with which we are entrusted, is another violation of the sentiment, frequently committed by people who would be very much astonished at being told they were not perfectly honest.

Is a deficiency of Concientiousness ever consistent with the enjoyment of a fair reputation?

Nothing is more common. Many who are not by nature

honest, act honestly in matters of business, because it is their interest to do so ; but such persons will be found constantly violating the minor branches of honesty, such as those mentioned, when no particular evil arises to themselves from the violation. Men previously considered honest, sometimes become bankrupt under disgraceful circumstances, involving their friends in one common ruin, and recklessly sacrificing, for the purpose of saving themselves, every human being on whom they can lay hold. This is the result of small Conscientiousness. So long as things go well, the man acts with integrity ; but when he finds that upright conduct will only hasten the crisis of his fate, his small modicum of Conscientiousness goes to sleep, and he has recourse to every dishonest expedient to put off the evil day.[72]

What is remorse?

That distressful state of mind arising from Conscientiousness or Benevolence when outraged. If a man, in an un-

[72] Every now and then, we hear of persons who had previously led an upright life, running off with large sums of money, to the no small astonishment of their friends, who are surprised at so unaccountable a change of character, as they term it. There is, however, no change of any kind. The individuals are, in every respect, precisely the same as they were before committing the felonious act; but they have been placed in different circumstances, and a seeming change is thus produced in their minds. If a young man, for instance, with moderate Conscientiousness is shopman to a linen draper, and obliged to account every night for the money which he draws in during the day, he may act with perfect honesty, as the temptation to steal is comparatively small, the produce of a single day's sale, being all he could possibly appropriate; but supposing him, in virtue of his sobriety, obliging disposition, attention to business, and dexterity in arithmetic, to be appointed head clerk to the establishment, and entrusted, from time to time, with large sums of money, it is perfectly possible that he may act very differently. His feeble sense of Conscientiousness may be unequal to the enormously increased temptation to which it is exposed, and nothing is more likely than that he should play the thief. This we hear of every day. Such cases would be far less frequent, or rather they would not happen at all, were the discriminative powers of Phrenology brought into play in the choice of confidential servants.

guarded moment, does any thing of which either of these faculties strongly disapproves, the pain arising from such disapproval constitutes remorse.

Do all who commit crimes feel the pangs of remorse?

They do not. Where Conscientiousness is very deficient, especially if Benevolence is in the same condition, no remorse whatever is experienced, though nothing is more common than the belief to the contrary, even among enlightened men. It is a great mistake to suppose that all the wicked are tortured by the pangs of conscience. Bellingham felt no remorse for the murder of Mr. Perceval, nor did Hare for his still more diabolical deeds.[73] When such wretches escape the gallows, they are more frequently punished by the abhorence of society than by any internal feeling arising from conscience. The mark of Cain is set upon them, and they walk the earth, outcasts from the human race.

[73] William Burke, whose Benevolence was not so small as that of Bellingham and Hare, though sadly overpowered by the predominance of his lower propensities, experienced the horrors of remorse to a great degree. He stated that, for a long time after the commission of his first murder, he felt it utterly impossible to banish for a single hour the recollection of the fatal struggle he had with his victim—the screams of distress and despair—the agonizing groans, and all the realities of the dreadful deed. At night, the bloody tragedy, accompanied by frightful visions of supernatural beings, tormented him in his sleep. For a long time, he shuddered on being alone in the dark, and during the night kept a candle constantly burning in his room. Even to the last, he could not overcome the repugnance of his moral nature to murder—such a glimmer of Benevolence as he had, was always in his way admonishing him; and this he had to extinguish in the fumes of whisky before he was able to overcome its influence. He positively asserted that he could not have committed murder when perfectly sober. In his head the organ of Conscientiousness was not so small as in most atrocious criminals—hence his visions of remorse.

The following is an instance of the absence of remorse. Many years ago, a wretch was broken upon the wheel at Lyons, for some shocking murders which he had committed. After having his limbs broken to pieces, the monster, just as he was expiring, laughed aloud, and upon being asked by the executioner what was the cause of his merriment, said he could not help feeling amused at the recollection of the grimaces made by a certain spoonmaker, into whose mouth he had poured melted tin.

In what class of persons is an ample endowment of Conscientiousness especially requisite?

No human being exists in whom a deficiency of this most god-like of all the faculties is not to be deplored. It is in a peculiar manner necessary, however, to judges on the bench, ministers of state, confidential servants, and all entrusted with onerous and important duties. Justice, in fact, is merely the manifestation of Conscientiousness.

Can this faculty be abused?

Yes, especially by weak-minded people. An honest man, for instance, if his understanding be so weak that he does not see the unjust tendency of an action, may persist in doing it, in the belief that he is really performing his duty. Another abuse of the faculty is an absurd adherence to pernicious principles which the person believes to be right. Excessive remorse and self-condemnation, where there are no circumstances to justify such feelings to half the extent in which they are experienced, are also abuses of Conscientiousness.

Do you affirm that all actions prompted by Conscientiousness are not necessarily just?

I do. This sentiment being a blind feeling, merely impels us to act justly and must be aided by the intellect in determining what is just. A man, for instance, may think that his action will realize the dictates of justice, whereas, had his intellect or knowledge been greater, he would have seen that the reverse would be the case.

Is great delight experienced in the exercise of this faculty?

Greater than perhaps from any other. " Honesty is its own reward." By acting in obedience to Conscientiousness, a man may involve himself in poverty, or meet with imprisonment and torture; still the consolation derived from his own integrity of purpose supports him : he is recompensed by the approval of his conscience, and rejoices even in the midst of suffering.[74]

17. HOPE.

Describe the position and function of this organ.

It lies on each side of Veneration, and its tendency is to produce the feeling of Hope. If the other faculties desire any thing, this one disposes us to believe in the possibility of their longings being gratified. An acquisitive person, for instance, will have a strong hope or expectation of being able to obtain money, should the faculty under consideration be powerful. Nor does this depend upon reflection; for when reason tells us that the chances are all the other way, we often continue hoping, and console ourselves with the idea of ultimate success.

What good purpose does this faculty serve?

It induces us to take gay and pleasant views of the future, and keeps up our spirits in the midst of misfortune: though clouds lower around us we are cheered with the expectation of speedy sunshine. Mungo Park in his desolate sojournings in Africa, and Sir John Ross in his miserable Polar solitude of four years, must have been powerfully supported by the influence of this organ. One of Ross's men died of sheer despondency, which would not have happened had he possessed the sentiment in vigour. The strong hope of a reprieve

---

[74] A beautiful instance of the power of Conscientiousness was witnessed by Dr. Smollett. Walking along the streets of Glasgow, a beggar, in great apparent misery, solicited charity of the doctor, who, putting his hand into his pocket, gave him what he supposed to be a shilling, but which was, in reality, a guinea. The beggar supposing that a mistake was committed, ran after his benefactor and tendered him the golden gift. "Good God!" exclaimed Smollett, on witnessing this act of integrity, "in what a habitation has honesty taken up her abode!" It need hardly be added that the generous novelist made this upright mendicant keep what he had received, as a reward for his admirable conduct.

has sustained the spirits of malefactors till within an hour of their being brought upon the scaffold. Mary M'Innes, while under sentence of death for murder, never lost the hope of being pardoned.

What is the result of a small organ of Hope?

The person is prone to despondency. He never takes cheering views of the future, and is surprised when any thing lucky occurs. People of this turn of mind are seldom disappointed, which is the only good that ever results from moderate Hope. In suicides, and those who view a future state with apprehension, we should expect the organ to be small in proportion to that of Cautiousness. Deficient Hope with large Cautiousness and Destructiveness predisposes to self-destruction.[75]

What are the abuses of Hope?

Rashness, credulity, and high expectations, not founded on reason. Those who "build castles in the air," gamblers, dabblers in lotteries and in the funds, are all much imbued with the sentiment of Hope.

What effect has Hope upon a person's religion?

It disposes to faith in agreeable views, and in particular to strong belief of a happy state of being in a life to come.

18. WONDER.

Where is the organ of Wonder situated?
Immediately above Ideality.
What is its function?

To inspire a love of the strange, the new, and the marvellous. It gives a fondness for supernatural stories, and a

---

[75] Suicide is sometimes hereditary. Dr. Gall mentions a family where the great-grandfather, the grandfather, and the father all destroyed themselves. Another he speaks of where the grandmother, her sister, and the mother did the same. The daughter attempted to throw herself out of a window, and the son hanged himself.

love of visiting mysterious and unfrequented countries; it also disposes to the belief in miracles, witches, and apparitions, and to superstition in general. It is not, however, the only source of the latter: ill directed and excessive Veneration, by disposing to belief in the assertions, however absurd, of revered authority, sometimes leads to superstitious opinions, especially when coupled with ignorance and weakness of intellect.

Name a few individuals in whom you would expect to find a large organ of Wonder.

I should look for it in such persons as Hoffmann, Radcliffe, Coleridge, and the Ettrick Shepherd. The Devils' Elixir, the Mysteries of Udolpho, Christabel, and Kilmenny, are all strongly characterised by the sentiment of Wonder.

Have persons who see apparitions, generally the organ large?

This fact seems to be well established. In the portraits of Tasso, who was visited by a familiar spirit, the organ appears large, giving his head that rounded fulness immediately above Ideality which is possessed by all who have a large development of the organ. It is very large in the head of Earl Grey, who is haunted by the apparition of a bloody head; and a crowd of cases have been collected by Dr. Gall and others, which seem to place the matter beyond a doubt. When Gall first saw Earl Grey, he said to a friend who stood by—" That man beholds visions." These facts are curious, and apparently incredible, but nevertheless they are supported by powerful evidence.

Why should a mere sentiment induce the seeing of visions, which is an intellectual operation?

The organ of Wonder cannot of itself do this, but it possesses the peculiar, though unaccountable, power of stimulating the perceptive organs, and thus exciting them to undue activity. Thus stimulated, they may conjure up false images and cause the person to imagine that he sees visions,

IDEALITY.

Is the organ peculiarly liable to excitement?

More so than most others. A fanatical preacher, by calling it into activity, will infect with his zeal a whole parish. Such was the case with Irving, Campbell, and other well-meaning but deluded enthusiasts—to say nothing of the notorious Joanna Southcote. During the persecutions in Scotland, excitement of this organ seems to have been exceedingly common among the Covenanters.

19. IDEALITY.

Where does this organ lie?

On the side of the head, over the temples. Above, it is bounded by Hope and Wonder, behind by Cautiousness, and below by Acquisitiveness. In the following likeness of the poet Tasso it is well developed.

What is the nature of the faculty connected with it?
It consists in a taste for the graceful, the beautiful, and

the sublime. All things which partake of these qualities gratify it. The savage desolation of Glenco, the awful gloom and sublimity of Chamouni, the graceful loveliness of Windermere, a beautiful woman, a lovely child, the Belvidere Apollo—all such objects stimulate the organ, and give rise to emotions of the grand or the beautiful. Painting, sculpture, and poetry, the loveliness of the moonlight hour, and the gorgeous majesty of sunset, are all dear to him who is gifted with Ideality.

Why, in some persons, is Ideality most highly gratified by the beautiful, in others by the sublime?

Destructiveness and Cautiousness, in combination with Ideality, are conjectured to give a love of the sublime in particular. Where a love of the beautiful predominates over that of the grand and the terrible, the two former are probably of more moderate dimensions. Destructiveness, which seems to take an interest in desolation, may give Ideality a bias towards the *dreary* sublime, while Cautiousness appears to be an ingredient in love of the *terrible*. The subject, however, stands in need of farther elucidation.

Will Ideality alone make a painter or a poet?

No; but it gives that imaginative feeling or enthusiasm which enters so largely into the composition of both. To excel in these arts other faculties are requisite; the painter requiring Form, Size, Colouring, and Constructiveness, and the poet Language, to embody his conceptions. Ideality, in conjunction with one or more of these intellectual faculties, produces what is called Imagination.

Mention a few individuals eminently gifted with Ideality.

Æschylus, Pindar, Shakspeare, Milton, Spenser, and Ariosto, among poets; Raphael, Michael Angelo, and Salvator Rosa among painters; Thorwalsden and Flaxman among sculptors. The works of these great men display the faculty in all its vigour.

What is the character of a person who has a great endowment of Ideality?

His language is generally elevated, his conceptions flow from him rapidly and eloquently, his conversation displays much richness, his illustrations are copious and varied, and he abounds in figurative language. This is peculiarly the case where the organs of Language and Comparison are also large. The style of Lord Bacon is replete with Ideality.

When the organ is small, is the character materially different?

Yes. The manners, thoughts, and conversation of the individual are homely and unadorned. He seldom or never uses poetical language. Grand or beautiful objects do not strike him forcibly, or throw him into raptures. He is a plain, matter-of-fact man, who boasts largely of his common sense, and affects a great contempt for poetry, and other imaginative productions. The organ is small in the heads of Locke, Mr. Joseph Hume, and Cobbett.[76]

Is the faculty sharpened or blunted by old age?

Age impairs Ideality more than almost any other faculty. Old people seldom display any of it, although there are very eminent exceptions, such as Homer, Milton, Goethe, and Titian.

---

[76] Cobbett's remarks on Milton are ludicrously characteristic of his deficient Ideality. "It has," says he, "become of late years the fashion to extol the virtues of potatoes, as it has been to admire the writings of Milton and Shakspeare. God, almighty and all fore-seeing, first permitting his chief angel to be disposed to rebel against him ; his permitting him to enlist whole squadrons of angels under his banners; his permitting the devils to bring cannon into this battle in the clouds ; his permitting one devil or angel, I forget which, to be split down the middle, from crown to crotch, as we split a pig; his permitting the two halves, intestines and all, to go slap up together again, and become a perfect body; his then permitting all the devil host to be tumbled headlong into a place called hell, of the local situation of which, no man can have an idea ; his causing gates (iron gates, too) to be erected to keep the devil in; his permitting him to get out, nevertheless, and to come and

What are the abuses of Ideality?

Extravagance of thought, absurd enthusiasm, flightiness, and a tendency to see every thing through a false medium. It requires strong reflecting powers, and much self-command, to restrain the ebullitions of excessive Ideality. Bombast, in speaking or writing, results from Ideality and Language, with deficient intellect. This kind of composition is very apt to impose upon people whose reflecting faculties are weak and knowledge very limited. With them it passes for true sublimity ; and the orator, preacher, or poet, who uses it is looked upon as a first-rate genius. The admiration in which the absurd rhapsodies of some clergymen, and the inflated effusions of many poetasters are held by a portion of the public, is a sufficient verification of this remark.

Is this a faculty, whose possession is to be envied?

Judging from the present condition of society, I should say that this is a doubtful point. Ideality certainly beautifies the mind, and gives rise to the most exquisite emotions ; but, unfortunately, dealing, as it does, with much that is imaginary, its possessor is apt to become disgusted with the grosser realities he must daily encounter. The refined sensibility which the faculty, when very active, bestows, is perhaps rather a curse ; and the occasional happiness resulting from it, frequently more than counterbalanced by the outrages which it meets with.

destroy the peace and happiness of his new creation; his permitting his son to take a pair of compasses out of a drawer, to trace the form of the earth; all this, and, indeed, the whole of Milton's poem, is such barbarous trash, so outrageously offensive to reason and to common sense, that one is naturally led to wonder, how it can have been tolerated by a people amongst whom astronomy, navigation, and chemistry are understood. But it is the fashion to turn up the eyes when 'Paradise Lost' is mentioned ; and if you fail herein, you want taste ; you want judgment even, if you do not admire this absurd and ridiculous stuff, when, if one of your relations were to write a letter in the same strain, you would send him to a mad-honse, and take his estate."

20. WIT.

Describe the situation of the organ of Wit.

It lies in the anterior, superior, and lateral parts of the forehead. The sketch here given of the head of Rabelais exhibits an ample development of it. The width of the upper part of his forehead is occasioned by the unusual size of the organ.

What is the nature of the faculty?

It may be described as that feeling which gives a tendency to view things in a ludicrous light, and inspires the sense of the ridiculous. Combined with Destructiveness, it leads to satire.

In whom would you expect to find the organ large?

In gay, mirthful, and facetious people; in those who possess the power of brilliant and humorous repartee, such as the celebrated Duchess of Gordon, Lady Wallace, Lord

Norbury, Harry Erskine; in such writers as the Rev. Sidney Smith, Sterne, Swift, Voltaire, Piron, and Cervantes; and in such actors as Garrick, Matthews, and Munden. Caricaturists, such as Hogarth, Bunbury, Rowlandson, and Cruikshank, must also be well endowed with the organ.

Is humour synonymous with wit?

It is not, although the best species of humour is that which is well seasoned with wit. Humour depends greatly upon the manner, wit not at all. A witty remark is witty all the world over, by whomsoever made, while what is humourous from one man, may be quite the reverse from another. "The School for Scandal" is a comedy remarkable for wit: "She Stoops to Conquer" is as remarkable for humour.

What follows when the organ is small?

The person has a natural dislike to drollery. Those who deal in it he considers buffons, and wit altogether as a piece of impertinence. He hates absurdity, and every thing which does not square with the most rigid common sense.

What are the abuses of the faculty?

An incessant tendency to laugh at every thing; an immoderate buoyancy and ebullience of spirits, and an inclination to say witty things on all occasions. Rabelais joked on his death-bed, and Sir Thomas More on the scaffold; proofs of the ruling passion being strong even in death. Wit is a most dangerous talent to be possessed by a badly-disposed person.

Are phrenologists agreed concerning the elementary function of this organ?

No: some are of opinion that it merely gives the ability to perceive differences, and that this perception is, in certain circumstances, attended with the emotion of the ludicrous. The faculty has not yet been satisfactorily analyzed.

21. IMITATION.

Describe the position and function of this organ.

It lies directly above Causality, and on each side of Benevolence. Its function is to produce imitation in general: mimicry is one of its most active results.

Is the imitative faculty peculiar to the human subject?

No. Some of the inferior animals are well endowed with it. The monkey, the parrot, the starling, and the mocking-bird, have the faculty in great perfection, as well as the organ which manifests it. Speaking of the mocking-bird, Dr. Mason Good observes, "Its own natural note is delightfully musical and solemn; but, beyond this, it possesses an instinctive talent of imitating the note of every other singing bird, and even the voice of every bird of prey, so exactly as to deceive the very kinds it attempts to mock. It is, moreover, playful enough to find amusement in the deception, and takes a pleasure in decoying smaller birds near it by mimicking their notes, when it frightens them almost to death, or drives them away with all speed, by pouring upon them the screams of such birds of prey as they most dread."

Do not other organs assist that of Imitation in producing mimicry?

Such undoubtedly is the case. Tune, for instance, adds much to the power of imitating voices and other sounds. Wit directs the imitative faculty in its own channel, and assists it greatly in pourtraying the ludicrous; while Secretiveness enables the mimic to veil his own peculiarities while representing those of another person. To imitate successfully coarse ferocious characters, Destructiveness and general large size of brain are necessary. Large Self-Esteem assists in representing pomposity, and large Love of Approbation in hitting off vanity. Ideality gives richness, beauty, and delicacy to imitations, while Individuality is very essential to a successful mimic, by the power of observation which it communicates.[77]

Is Imitation necessary for the profession of an actor?

Eminently so. The process by which the performer merges his own character in that represented, is effected by means of Imitation and Secretiveness. All distinguished actors are good mimics, even in the vulgar sense of the word. Such was the case with Garrick, Foote, Kean, and a multitude of others. Matthews, who was one of the best ever known, had a large organ of Imitation. It is found greatly developed in good ventriloquists.

Is it requisite for any other profession?

It is very necessary for painters—painting, especially portraiture, being essentially an imitative art. Most good painters excel in mimicry, and this results from the great degree in which they are gifted with the organ. Dramatic writers require a large endowment of it. In the likenesses of Shakspeare—whether these be authentic or not—it appears greatly developed, and so, also, it was in the head of Sir Walter Scott, whose writings are highly dramatic.

Must a person with large Imitation be necessarily a good mimic?

No. The imitative talent may display itself in some higher walk than in mere mimicry, as in those mentioned above.

---

[77] The power of a combination of organs in producing mimicry of the first order, is well displayed in a gentleman well known to me, and distinguished for the brilliancy and versatility of his talents. The organs of Imitation and Secretiveness are greatly developed in his head. Tune is well marked, and he has a very fine endowment of Individuality, Wonder, Ideality, and Wit. Benevolence and Love of Approbation are very large; and there is also a large Destructiveness. The head is of great general size, and the temperament an extremely active one. In harmony with this combination, he possesses mimetical talents of the highest order. He is,

ORDER II.—INTELLECTUAL FACULTIES.

What faculties are called Intellectual?

Those which make man and the lower animals acquainted with the existence, qualities, and relations of objects. They are divided, though not quite accurately as to details, into three Genera,—1st, The External Senses; 2d, The Internal Senses or Perceptive Faculties; and 3d, The Reflective Faculties.

GENUS I.—THE EXTERNAL SENSES.

What are the External Senses?

Those faculties which, by means of organs in direct relation with the external world, are the inlets of impressions or sensations from without. Some object to calling the

---

moreover, an admirable ventriloquist; and his displays in this walk have a beauty and supernatural effect—the result of large Ideality and Wonder—which I have not heard equalled. His large Benevolence enables him to represent successfully good-humoured, his large Wit ridiculous, and his large Love of Approbation vain characters. His good endowment of Destructiveness aids him greatly in representing anger and ferocity; and the general size of his brain gives him the power of infusing energy and boldness, when these are required, into his imitations. In addition to his multifarious accomplishments as a mimic, he possesses incredible power over his face, which he can mould into a variety of different aspects, each accurately representing a real character; and so totally unlike are these from one another, that while some are striking likenesses of people of twenty-five or thirty, others correctly resemble men of fourscore. These changes of face add immensely to the effect of his imitations, more especially as he gives, along with each particular physiognomy, the exact voice of the person whose face is represented. His power of transmuting himself, as it were, into other characters, is, indeed, altogether astonishing; and for brilliancy, variety, intensity, and sustained power, I never saw any one whose imitative talents could be put into competition with his. A few of the numerous Protean aspects of this incomparable mimic have been sketched for me in a very spirited manner, by my friend Mr. Macnee, Portrait Painter in Glasgow.

External Senses intellectual faculties. In answer to this, it may be stated, that a faculty is a power, and intellectual faculties are those which know. The sense of feeling knows. It perceives and discriminates sensations of a particular kind. True, the nerves do not perceive, but let it be remembered, that the senses have cerebral organs, probably at the base of the brain. Mutilating experiments seem to prove, that if the parts about the medulla oblongata are allowed to remain, the senses continue active, notwithstanding the removal of the hemispheres. As each external sense must have a cerebral organ, there is thus no absurdity in considering them to be intellectual faculties.

How many senses are there?

Hitherto their number has been limited to five, viz. Feeling or Touch, Taste, Smell, Hearing, and Sight; but good reason has recently been shown for regarding certain nerves distributed to the muscles, and discovered by Sir Charles Bell, as having reference to a sixth sense—that of Mechanical Resistance. The following explanation will give some idea of this sense:—To enable the muscles to execute the mandates of the will, they are connected with the brain by the nerves of motion, which are every where distributed over them. Till very recently, these nerves of motion were supposed to be simple; but Sir Charles Bell has demonstrated, that, in reality, each is composed of two nerves, bound up in the same sheath, but serving different purposes. One, called the Motor nerve, transmits from the brain to the muscle the nervous stimulus necessary to produce the desired contraction and, consequently, motion; while the other, that of the sense of Mechanical Resistance, gives the brain information as to the state of the muscle whose contraction is desired, thus enabling the brain to send to it the exact amount of nervous stimulus necessary for accomplishing the intended effort. By " the state of the muscles," is meant the existing degree of their contraction—in other words, the force which they are exerting against a resisting body.[78]

Is it the brain which takes cognizance of impressions, or are they perceived by these external organs of the senses?

The brain undoubtedly. The external organs have no function, but to convey the impressions to the sensorium.

How is this reconcileable with the fact, that when the nerve of sight is impaired, vision is destroyed?

The cause is obvious, for if the communicating medium which carries the impression to the brain is destroyed, it is not to be supposed that the brain can receive the impression.

Does the brain ever receive, by other means, impressions similar to those brought to it by the senses?

It occasionally does, but the impressions are false, and have no relation to any thing occurring, or existing, without. Thus, in consequence of some internal stimulus operating in the brain, the blind have sometimes a distinct impression of seeing, and the deaf of hearing. The brain, in such cases, is stimulated in the same way as by the eyes and ears bringing impressions to it, but those external senses being incapable of carrying such impressions, the perceptions are, of course, fallacious. It sometimes happens, in like manner, that people neither blind nor deaf see apparitions and hear sounds that have no existence without. This occurs in consequence of the brain or nerves being affected by disease, in the same way as they are influenced in health by external impressions.

---

[78] See a very able and elaborate essay by Mr. Simpson, in the 43d Number of the Phrenological Journal, where the functions of the motor nerve, and nerve of mechanical resistance, are clearly and satisfactorily distinguished and illustrated.

GENUS II.—THE PERCEPTIVE, OR KNOWING FACULTIES.

SPECIES I.—INTELLECTUAL FACULTIES WHICH TAKE COGNIZANCE OF THE EXISTENCE OF EXTERNAL OBJECTS AND THEIR PHYSICAL QUALITIES.

22. INDIVIDUALITY.

Describe the position of this organ.

It lies in the centre and lower part of the forehead, immediately above the root of the nose. Both it and Locality are represented as largely developed in the following sketch of the head of Pope Martin V.:—

22. Individuality.   27. Locality.

What is the nature of its faculty?

To give an aptitude for observing and remembering objects, without any reference to their qualities, or the purposes served by them. For instance, two persons, one with a large, the other with a small development, enter a room together: the first notices every thing presented to his senses—the chairs, the pictures, the ornaments—and remembers accurately what he sees; the other has little tendency of the kind. Objects do not strike him with any thing like the same force, although he may be otherwise a very superior man. Farther, it gives the memory of facts which are not events. It recollects, for example, that platina is heavier than gold, that salt water supports bodies better than fresh, that the tower of Strasburgh cathedral is very high, and so on. If we read Peregrine Pickle, it will enable us to remember that Jack Hatchway had a wooden leg, and that Commodore Trunnion was blind of an eye, but the power of recollecting the varied adventures of these characters depends on another organ—that of Eventuality.

To what class of persons is a good endowment of Individuality especially useful?

It is a valuable faculty to the naturalist, the physician, the lawyer, and merchant—to all, in short, who are obliged to load their memory with numerous details.

What is the character of those who have the organ large?

They are clever observant persons, with a great aptitude for remembering such facts as we have mentioned. Nothing escapes them; but they are often incapable of reasoning upon the knowledge they possess, and very frequently shallow; reflection and profundity depending upon a higher order of faculties.[79] A man who has Individuality and

---

[79] " I accompanied two gentlemen to see a great public work, in one of whom Individuality was large, and Causality small, and in the other of whom the proportions of these organs were reversed. The former, in surveying the different objects and operations, put question after question to the workmen in rapid and long-continued succession; and nearly all the information which he carried away with him was acquired in answer to

good reflective organs combined, will be both a quick observer and a deep thinker. Watt seems to have been a person of this stamp, and Cuvier was another illustrious example.

Are nations variously endowed with this organ?

Its size varies much in different nations: it is smaller in the English than in the French head, and in the Scotch smaller than in either. The quickness of observation and aptitude for details possessed by the French, depend upon the ample endowment which the nation enjoys of this organ.

Do not the frontal sinuses[80] prove an obstacle to the accurate ascertainment of the size of Individuality?

In the cases of adults and old people, where the sinuses are large and approximate closely, they do. The best way to ascertain the dimensions of the organ, is to examine the heads of young people before the sinuses are formed. Even in adults, however, deficiency of the organ can never be mistaken.

---

specific interrogatories. His mind scarcely supplied a step by its own reflection; and did not appear to survey the operations as a systematic whole. The latter individual looked a long time in silence before he put a question at all; and when he did ask one, it was, What is the use of that? The answer enabled his own mind to supply a multitude of additional ideas; he proceeded in his examination, and it was only on arriving at another incomprehensible part of the apparatus that he again inquired. At last he got through; then turned back, and, with the most apparent satisfaction, contemplated in silence the operations from beginning to end as an entire system. I heard him afterwards describe what he had seen, and discovered that he had carried off a distinct comprehension of the principles and objects of the work. It is probable, that a superficial observer would have regarded the first as the acute, intelligent, and observing man of genius—the person who noticed every thing, and asked about every thing; and the latter as a dull uninteresting man, who put only two or three questions, looked heavily, and said nothing."—*Combe's System*, 4th edition, vol. ii. p. 582.

80 The frontal sinuses are two hollow spaces—one on each side—above the root of the nose, formed by the receding of the outer from the inner table of the skull.

23. FORM.

Where is the organ of Form situated?

On each side of the crista galli[81] of the ethmoid bone: it gives width between the eyes, as may be seen in the heads of artists who are eminent for portraiture. Audubon, in describing the person of Bewick, the celebrated engraver in wood, represents his eyes as being placed farther apart from each other than those of any other man he had ever seen; and, in accordance with their formation, Bewick's works indicate a very admirable perception of form. The following engraving of Vandyke's head represents a large development of the organ :—

What faculty is connected with this organ?

[81] A small perpendicular projection arising from the upper surface of the ethmoid bone. The olfactory nerve, or nerve of smell, lies on each side of the crista galli.

That of perceiving and recollecting forms. People differ wonderfully in this respect. One man from taking a glance at an object will sketch it accurately: another could not give a correct representation were he to labour for a month. It is a most material element in the talent for drawing; it enables us to take likenesses, and is, in fact, absolutely essential to artists of every description. The organ gives the power of recollecting faces; of this, George III. was a good illustration. It also tends, especially if accompanied with an active Comparison, to the personification of abstract ideas; representing, for instance, time under the symbol of an hour glass, or an old man with a scythe, innocence as a dove, sin as a serpent, death as a skeleton, and so on. It enables the architect to produce noble designs; and by its aid milliners, mantua-makers, and tailors invent patterns, and thus add to the varieties of dress.

In what nations is it large?

It is large in the Chinese, which accounts for the minute, and almost frivolous accuracy, of their delineations. It is large also in the French, and, I should suppose, in the Italian head.

24. SIZE.

Describe the situation and function of this organ.

It lies over the inner angle of the eye, immediately above the root of the nose. Its faculty is to give the idea of space, and the power of appreciating the dimensions of objects; in other words, the quantity of space which they occupy. It takes cognizance also of lineal space, or distance. At first sight, the function of this organ may seem to be involved in that of the preceding; but Size is really a different faculty from that which perceives forms. We may have a very perfect idea of the shape of a body, and a most inaccurate one of its bulk. Ask one man the length of a certain log of wood, and he will tell you with considerable accuracy by merely looking at it; ask another, and he errs egregiously. This shows that there must be a special organ for Size.

Is a good development useful to an artist?

It is, by enabling him to give each part of the representation its proper size; in other words, to keep the proportions accurate. To the landscape-painter it is probably of great use, the accurate perception of perspective being supposed to depend upon it. To artizans and mechanics in general, it must be a matter of importance to have a correct idea of size. Those in whom the faculty is weak, will constantly require to have recourse to compasses and other measuring instruments, for the purpose of adjusting the respective dimensions of what they are engaged upon.

25. WEIGHT.

What is the peculiar function of this organ?

The organ of Weight, which adjoins, and lies to the outside of Size, is supposed to give the idea of the ponderosity of bodies, and, in general, of mechanical force and resistance. It is probably to this organ that the nerves of mechanical resistance convey the idea of the state of the muscles. If it is largely developed, that idea, so communicated, will be proportionally vivid.

In whom is it said to be large?

In those who excel in archery, skating, quoits, and all who have great facility in judging of momentum and resistance in mechanics. It is probably large in the heads of skilful pugilists, such as Randal, Ward, and Belcher; also in those who excel in fencing, such as Roland and Foucart, and in good equestrians and rope-dancers, as, for instance,

Ducrow, in whom it is amply developed. Children who walk early are supposed to have it large. It is well marked in the heads of eminent engineers, and all who have a talent for the investigation of mechanical forces. Sir Isaac Newton, Sir David Brewster, Sir John Leslie, and Mr. Jardine of Edinburgh, the eminent engineer, afford instances in which it is strikingly developed. It is supposed by some, to give the idea of the perpendicularity of bodies; at least, several builders who possess this power in great perfection, are observed to have it large. This and the preceding organ are not so well established[82] as some others, and farther observations are still wanting to place them beyond the pale of probability. The existence of the faculties, however, seems unquestionable.

26. COLOURING.

What is the nature of this faculty?

To communicate the perception of colours. When the organ is large, this perception is extremely vivid. There is a love of colours for their own sake, and a remarkable power of minutely discriminating their nicest shades. Combined with Ideality, it gives a just and delicate perception of colours. When the organ is small, a difficulty is experienced in perceiving and distinguishing colours, and in appreciating their harmony. Such cases are often met with, and arise from a defective size of this part of the brain. Many people cannot distinguish brown from olive,

---

82 When we say that an organ is not well established, it is not to be understood that we infer there is any faculty without a corresponding organ, but simply, that phrenologists are yet undecided, whether the cerebral part they have been led to regard as the organ, is the just one. If there be a faculty of Weight, there must be an organ: whether the organ which has been assigned as the seat of this faculty be the real one, future observations must determine.

green from blue, or yellow from orange; while others, though not so defective as this, are unable to perceive harmony or discord in the arrangement or combination of colours.[83]

May not this depend upon indifferent sight?

It has nothing to do with this, because the persons so circumstanced have, as respects every thing else, as good eyes as their neighbours. Many people hear perfectly well, and yet cannot distinguish one tune from another: it is the same with the eyes, as regards colours.

Where is the organ situated?

At the middle of the eyebrows, between the organs of Weight and Order. Its position may be seen in the annexed likeness of Rubens, in whose head it was very large.

[83] "Dr. Nicol has recorded a case, where a naval officer purchased a blue uniform coat and waistcoat, with red breeches to match the blue, and Mr. Harvey describes the case of a tailor at Plymouth, who, on one occasion,

In what class of persons is this organ large?

In artists distinguished for colouring, as Rubens, Titian, Claude Lorraine, and Salvator Rosa, and in individuals who have a passion for brilliant and gaudy dresses. Those who are particularly fond of flowers and of birds with beautiful plumage, have probably the organ large: it is very ample in Montreuil, author of the "French Florist." Poets who are fond of describing the infinite hues presented by nature, are well endowed with it.

In which sex is it generally larger?

In the female. Women, as colourists, have rivalled men, while for design and the higher walks of painting, they are greatly inferior. The passion for gaudy ornaments is, besides, stronger in them than in the other sex.[84]

SPECIES II.—INTELLECTUAL FACULTIES WHICH TAKE COGNIZANCE OF THE RELATIONS OF EXTERNAL OBJECTS.

27. LOCALITY.

May not a large frontal sinus be mistaken for this organ?

repaired an article of dress with crimson instead of black silk, and on another, patched the elbow of a blue coat with a piece of crimson cloth. It deserves to be remarked, that our celebrated countryman, the late Mr. Dugald Stewart, had a similar difficulty in distinguishing colours, and the same remark applies to Messrs. Dalton and Troughton. Mr. Stewart discovered this defect, when one of his family was admiring the beauty of the Siberian crab-apple, which he could not discover from the leaves, but by its form and size. Mr. Dalton cannot distinguish blue from pink. Mr. Troughton regards red, ruddy pinks, and brilliant oranges as yellows, and greens as blues, so that he is capable only of appreciating blue and yellow colours."
—*Sir David Brewster's Letters on Natural Magic*, p. 31.

[84] The organ of Colouring in persons born blind, or who have lost their sight in infancy, is always deficient. This was first observed by Dr. Spurzheim, and I had an opportunity of verifying the fact during a visit, which I made along with Mr. Combe, to the Glasgow Blind Asylum. The organ never having been exercised, ceases to grow. It is perfectly reasonable to infer, that the same law prevails with respect to other organs.

It may; and cases, doubtless, have occurred, where such a circumstance has led to mistakes : but, generally speaking, the sinus does not ascend higher than the inferior portion of Locality; and in children, at any rate, a mistake of this kind cannot well occur, as the sinus, at that age, is scarcely ever formed. In the case of adults, no prudent phrenologist gives an unqualified opinion as to the size of this organ, except where the flatness or depression of the surface unequivocally proclaims it to be small.

How may a large sinus be generally discriminated from the organ?

The prominences formed by the sinus are irregular in form, and lie for the most part horizontally; the elevations occasioned by large Locality are uniform in shape, and extend obliquely upwards, towards the middle of the forehead.

What is the nature of the faculty connected with this organ?

Locality takes cognizance of the relative positions of objects;[85] it bestows a great aptitude for remembering places

---

[85] "An individual well known in London by the name of 'Memory-Corner Thomson,' is remarkable for an astonishing local memory. In the space of twenty-four hours, and at two sittings, he drew a correct plan of the whole parish of St. James, with several streets belonging to the parishes of Marylebone, St. Ann, and St. Martin. This plan contained all the squares, streets, lanes, courts, passages, markets, churches, chapels, public buildings, houses, stables, angles of houses, and a great number of other objects, as wells, parapets, stones, trees, &c., and an exact plan of Carlton House and St. James' Palace. He executed all this without the aid of any plan, without compasses, without books, or any other data. He made out also, from memory, an exact plan of the parish of St. Andrew, and he offered to do the same with that of St. Giles in the fields, St. Paul, Covent Garden, St. Clement, and Newchurch. If a particular house in any given street was mentioned, he would at once tell what trade was carried on in it, the position and appearance of the shop, and its contents. In going through a large hotel, completely furnished, he is able to retain every thing, and make an inventory from memory; but a dialogue, on the other hand, that he may have heard, even two or three times, will be quite new to him in the course of two or three days."— *Phrenological Journal,* vol. iv. p. 356.

where we have once been, and a fondness for travelling. Persons who have it large seldom lose their way, and when they have once been at a place, can return to it with peculiar facility.

In what class of persons is the organ large?

In distinguished voyagers and travellers, such as Columbus, Vasco de Gama, Captain Cook, and Mungo Park; and, accordingly, in the likenesses of these eminent men, it appears amply developed. It is large, also, in great geographers and astronomers, such as Malte Brun, Kepler, Galileo, Tycho Brahé, and Newton. Authors who describe, and artists who delineate scenery well, have also a good development. It appears large in Julius Cæsar, Michael Angelo, Tasso, Sir Walter Scott, Professor Wilson, Breugel the landscape-painter, and M. Jaubert, Professor of Oriental Languages at the Bibliothèque du Roi, whose passion for travelling is excessive. In the sketch of Pope Martin, page 122, the organ is seen to be greatly developed. It is large in the American Indians, and other nomadic tribes; and it appears highly probable, that the continued exercise to which it is subjected in these people, actually increases its size.

Have the lower animals the faculty?

Yes. Dogs, by means of Locality, trace their steps homewards, even for hundreds of miles. The same faculty it is which directs birds in their periodical migrations, and the carrier-pigeon in its extensive flights. The way, however, in which it acts in the lower animals, is often very obscure, and, indeed, perfectly inexplicable. A dog, for instance, has been sent many hundred miles by sea, and has returned over land to the very spot at which it embarked. There have not been awanting instances where the faculty has operated on the human subject in a somewhat similar way, and without the concurrence of sight. Metcalf, the blind traveller, was an instance of the kind. This remarkable man, if once in a place, could readily find his way back again: indeed, we every day observe blind men walking alone, and in perfect safety, through the most crowded streets, guided, doubtless, in their gloomy path, by the mysterious influence of Locality.[86]

What are the abuses of Locality?

An excessive tendency to ramble about, and a total incapacity for remaining long in one place. This is sometimes so strong, as almost to amount to a disease. Such was the case with the Abbé Dabrowki of Prague, in whose head the organ of Locality was enormously large. Dr. Gall met, one day, at Vienna, a woman, in whom the development was so great as to amount to a deformity. In her, also, the passsion for rambling and visiting foreign countries was extreme.

28. NUMBER.

Describe the situation and function of this organ.

It lies at the external angle of the eye, and when large, swells out the frontal bone at that particular spot, and likewise, occasionally, gives the outer extremity of the eyebrow an overhanging and drooping appearance. The function connected with it is that which gives the power of arithmetical calculation. Great differences exist among individuals

---

[86] "It is common," says Mr. John Alston, in his Report of the Blind Asylum at Glasgow, "for adults who reside in distant parts of the city to come to their employment without a guide. In farther proof of their capability of walking without an assistant, a young boy of fourteen years of age, whose parents resided six miles from Glasgow, was in the habit of visiting them. He was accustomed to leave the establishment without an attendant, traverse the whole length of the city, finding his way through the Calton, Bridgeton, along Rutherglen bridge, through that town and to his father's house. This he did with as much correctness as if he had been in full possession of vision." I am farther informed by the teacher of the asylum, himself an intelligent blind man, that one of the inmates actually walked, without a guide, as far as his native place Strathaven, a distance from Glasgow of seventeen miles.

as respects the strength of this faculty. Some men can solve, with little effort, the most difficult questions in arithmetic: others can hardly manage the simplest, let them labour as they please.

Mention a few individuals remarkable for a large development of the organ.

Zerah Colburn, the American calculating boy, George Bidder, and Jedediah Buxton—all of them distinguished for their extraordinary arithmetical talents, are instances in point. The same remark applies to Playfair, Leslie, Inigo Jones, Wren, Hutton, Euler, and Kepler: and these distinguished men were all remarkable for the extent to which they possessed the computative faculty. The annexed likeness of Jedediah Buxton represents the appearance often presented by a large development of the organ.[87]

[87] Some calculating boys lose their arithmetical talent when they grow up. Such was the case with a relative of my own, who at the age of seven possessed great natural capabilities in this way, but in four or five years he

Is this organ larger in some nations than in others?

It is. In the Negro and Esquimaux head the organ is small, and these people are generally very deficient in arithmetical talent. Humboldt mentions, that the Chaymas, a South American tribe, have great difficulty in comprehending any thing which belongs to numercial relation. He says, that he never saw a man among them who might not be made to say that he was eighteen or sixty years of age; and he adds, that the corner of the eye is sensibly raised up towards the temple. Wafer observed the same remarkable want of calculating power among the Indians at the Isthmus of Darien.

May this faculty coexist vigorously with a weak general intellect?

This may undoubtedly happen. The best arithmetician I ever knew was a man of a very feeble understanding; and even idiots are sometimes excellent computists. Knowing this fact, it is very wrong to accuse people of being dull or stupid, merely because it so happens that they are incapable of learning arithmetic. Some men of distinguished talent cannot even master the multiplication-table; and one of the first phrenologists and philosophical writers of the present day is so deficient in the computative faculty as to be unable to add up his own cash-book. In Dr. Gall, likewise, this talent was exceedingly feeble. Fossati observes, that he never saw him master a process in simple multiplication or division that was at all complicated.

---

lost them, and is now a very indifferent calculator. Zerah Colburn, too, is an instance of the same kind. "Previous to the wonderful manifestations of arithmetical power exhibited by young Colburn, he had been afflicted with chorea, and was at the time very nervous, and sometimes evidently suffered pain when called on to exhibit his powers; and when he recovered his health he lost his extraordinary calculating powers."—*Practical Phrenology, by Silas Jones*, Boston, 1836.—I have little doubt that Colburn's organ of Number was overworked, and thus rendered apathetic.

Will a large organ of Number make a person a good mathematician?

No: other faculties are necessary, although Number is a very useful one. It was thought, that some calculating boys, from the force of their arithmetical powers, would have excelled in mathematics, but the result did not correspond with the anticipation. As mathematics treat of configuration and space or dimension, as well as of number, the organs of Form and Size are indispensable to eminence in that department.

Is this faculty possessed by animals?

The point has never been correctly ascertained. Some philosophers imagine that the magpie possesses the power of computation to a certain extent. Le Roy, for instance, supposes, that the creature counts three, while Dupont de Nemours extends its talents, in this respect, as far as nine. Such assertions, however, must be based on little better than conjecture.[88]

29. ORDER.

Where is this organ situated?

It lies between Colouring and Number, and is marked 20 in the bust.

What is its function?

To bestow a love of order and arrangement. When the organ is very large, there is a punctilious nicety about the manner in which things are placed, and the order in which they are done. The person is annoyed by confusion, and apt to be dainty and finical. He is an ardent admirer of the well known maxims, " Say every thing in its proper way;

---

[88] It is said that a dog must have this faculty, because it discovers if one of its young has been removed; but this, as Spurzheim remarks, it may perceive from the want of the individual so carried away, without counting the number of the whole.

put every thing in its proper place; and do every thing in its proper time." His minute love of arrangement is not less annoying to those in whom the faculty is feeble, than their want of systematic regularity is to him. When the faculty is weak the reverse is the case, and there is a marked indifference to order and arrangement. Confusion and want of neatness give no annoyance: the person is apt to be careless in his dress, disorderly in his household, and, unless his Conscientiousness be strong, unpunctual to appointments.

To what class of persons is a large organ of Order especially useful?

To the mistress of a family, and particularly to domestic servants: it is essential to keepers of museums, to gardeners, and all who have the charge of establishments of any kind.

Is the organ large in authors distinguished for the precision and order of their writings ?

Not necessarily: its powers seem to be confined to physical arrangement. Causality and Comparison are the chief systematizers. Such authors as Linnæus and Cuvier, were indebted to these organs, and not to the one under review, for their great power of classification.

30. EVENTUALITY.

Describe the position and function of this organ.

It lies in the centre of the forehead, above Individuality; and gives the power of recollecting events and phenomena. Books that abound in incident, such as Don Quixote, Robinson Crusoe, Gulliver's Travels, and Roderick Random, are characterised by marked Eventuality; and persons who have the faculty strong, will remember vividly the occurrences related in such works. These persons are considered clever, in the common meaning of the term: they pick up a knowledge of events readily, although it may so happen that they are perfectly unable to reason thereupon, or turn it to any proper use.

Does Eventuality assist in acquiring a language?

No; but it will enable us to recollect any particular events recorded in that language. The power of acquiring languages depends on a special organ.

What does inquisitiveness depend upon?

Upon Eventuality and Individuality in excess, generally combined with Wonder. If Secretiveness is conjoined, the inquisitive tendency will be still greater.

Will a person with large Eventuality, be necessarily inquisitive?

Not in the common acceptation of the term, which is usually employed to designate a species of impertinence. If his reflecting powers be deficient, he will be apt to show a meddling, inquisitive turn about paltry matters; if strong, he will despise this, and direct the faculty to the acquisition of really useful knowledge. Still, it is the same power at work, only in the one case employed about trifles, in the other on matters of importance.

From what does gossip arise?

From large Eventuality and Language, with small Secretiveness. The person has a great craving to know every thing which is going on, and an equally great craving to divulge it: he is constantly talking of the affairs of his neighbours. Gossips have almost always small brains, and are destitute of a liberal education. A large-brained and well educated person, despises the paltry habit of retailing all the chit-chat which he hears, and is not likely to become addicted to this vice. Self-Esteem is often strongly manifested by gossips, who are generally envious, jealous creatures.

Illustrate by some examples the difference between Individuality and Eventuality.

Individuality concerns itself with what exists, Eventuality

with what happens. Substantive nouns express the objects of the former, active verbs those of the latter. When I say that Lord John Russel is a little man, that the Duke of Wellington has a Roman nose, or that camels have humps upon their backs, it is Individuality which suggests these remarks: when, however, I observe that after being challenged by Sir Robert Peel, Mr. O'Connell contrived to get himself arrested, and then made a vow in heaven never to fight duels; that the Houses of Parliament were burned in consequence of overheating the flues; or that Earl Spenser rears the fattest cattle in England, then the observations are suggested by Eventuality. We may in another manner exhibit the operation of the two faculties. If I see a sportsman standing in a field with his gun levelled, an object is presented to my Individuality. If he draws the trigger, discharges the gun, and kills a bird, these are all occurrences or events in the process of active operation, and are recognised by Eventuality.

31. TIME.

Where is the organ of Time situated?

In the middle region of the forehead, on each side of Eventuality. It is not considered to be fully established, but the existence of the faculty is sufficiently manifest.

What talent depends upon the organ?

The perception of duration, or time. It enables those who are well endowed with it, to keep time in dancing and in music, to judge accurately of the intervals which elapse between given periods, and to conjecture the hour of the day with comparative precision, without consulting the clock: it is essential to good versification. People differ in all these particulars, and the differences depend on the degree in which they are gifted with this organ.

140   TUNE.

Mention some other ways in which Time may manifest itself.
In the accuracy with which a regiment of soldiers fires at the word of command; or goes through the manual and platoon exercise, by observing the movements of the fugleman. In those who keep bad time in performing such exercises the faculty is feeble. It is also feeble in those who acquire with difficulty the art of dancing, and the same remark applies to bad timists in music.

32. TUNE.

Where does this organ lie?
In the lateral portion of the forehead, outside of Time, and immediately above Order and Number. The position

of the organ is shown in the annexed portrait of Handel, in whose head it was greatly developed.

What function is connected with it?

The feeling for music, and, when accompanied with Time, Imitation, &c., the talent for playing on instruments, or singing with skill and success. It is large in all who have a decided musical genius, such as Glück, Weber, Rossini, Malibran, Catalani, and Pasta.[89]

Is it confined to the human species?

No: birds have the organ and its accompanying faculty. It is distinctly marked in the nightingale, the thrush, the linnet, and other singing birds. It is larger in the head of the male singing bird than in the female, which accounts for the superior power of song possessed by the former. In birds which do not sing, it is not similarly developed. If we compare the head of the hawk, the crow, or the eagle, with those of the tribe of songsters, the difference will at once appear obvious in the region of Tune.

May not the inability of certain birds to sing, depend upon the unsuitable organization of the throat?

This objection has no force; because whenever nature has bestowed the talent for any thing, she has, at the same time, endowed the animal with the apparatus for exercising that talent. If the raven had the cerebral organization of the nightingale, nature, which does nothing in vain, would have given it the vocal apparatus for song.[90] The hawk is

---

[89] "The faculty gives the perception of melody; but this is only one ingredient in a genius for music. Time is requisite to give a just perception of intervals, Ideality to communicate elevation and refinement, and Secretiveness and Imitation to produce expression; while Constructiveness, Form, Weight, and Individuality, are necessary to supply mechanical expertness:—qualities all indispensable to a successful performer. Even the largest organ of Tune will not enable its possessor to play successfully on the harp, if Weight be deficient; the capacity of communicating to the string the precise vibratory impulse requisite to produce each particular note will then be wanting."—*Combe's System, 4th edition*, vol. ii. p. 533.

[90] An ingenious friend has stated in objection to this, that some men have great musical talent, and yet cannot sing well, for want of good voice.

a ferocious, sanguinary animal, and it is armed accordingly with formidable claws, and a powerful beak, wherewith to exercise its particular instincts. Of what use would such armoury be to a timid creature like the dove? or what would the hawk be, were it weaponless like the dove? In such a case, the lust for blood and thirst for destroying, which have been bestowed for the purpose of gratification, would be unaccompanied with any means of carrying these intentions of nature into effect.

Is there any reason to suppose, that the British will ever equal the Germans and Italians in music?

None. The organ in the British head is decidedly smaller, so that, although an individual may now and then arise, capable of contesting the palm with the Haydns, the Rossinis, and the Handels, still, as a people, they can never compete with these nations in musical talent. It is a common remark that their deficiency of talent for music, is owing to the taste for this accomplishment never having been sufficiently cultivated in Great Britain: but why has it not been so cultivated? Simply because the British are not emi-

---

Such an objection, however, is more specious than solid. The chief purpose of voice is speech, and man is not, like the nightingale, merely a singing animal, or, like the hawk, merely an animal formed for destructive purposes. Supposing a man to have a good development of Tune, together with an indifferent voice, it cannot be said that his musical talent is thrown away upon him, and that, because he cannot sing, he cannot turn it to good purpose. Man has faculties which have enabled him to invent and construct instruments, from which he draws music far surpassing in sublimity and beauty, that of his own voice. I am not aware that Weber or Beethoven could sing well; yet what exquisite delight did not these men derive from their organ of Tune, and what wonderful works did it not stimulate them to produce? Another consideration is, that while birds, by living in accordance with the laws of nature, have their functions, and among others the voice, in a comparatively perfect condition, man, whose unnatural mode of life, and disregard of these laws, have tended much to injure his capabilities, does not generally enjoy that perfection of the vocal power, which, had he acted in accordance with the organic laws, he probably would have possessed.

nently musical. If the national talent lay decidedly in this particular walk, they would naturally cultivate it, and be able to cope with the Germans and Italians.

Would you expect the organ large in every good performer on a musical instrument?

No. A fair development, aided by an active temperament and great perseverance, may make a very good performer indeed; but one of the highest order, such as Paganini, requires an ample organ of Tune. To eminent original composers, as Mozart, Haydn, and Auber, a large development is indispensable.[91]

On what do differences of taste in music depend?

On the state of the other organs. A person whose Veneration and Tune are both large, will naturally prefer sacred music: large Combativeness and Tune will induce a preference to martial music, and so on.

Is the organ of Tune fully established?

The facts in support of it are so numerous, that this appears to be the case. The discrimination of the size of the organ is, however, so difficult, that, except in cases of extreme development or deficiency, mistakes are frequently committed in estimating it. This is particularly the case with sciolists in Phrenology, who are disposed to make a display of their skill more frequently with regard to this

---

[91] A lady incidentally, and without any reference to Phrenology, informed me, that her female servant could not distinguish one tune from another, although her hearing was perfect. She farther mentioned, as a curious circumstance, that the woman was constantly committing mistakes when the bells rung, as she was unable to distinguish the door bell from the dining-room one, although every other person in the family could do so with ease, so very different were the tones of the two bells. On examining the woman's head, I found the organ of Tune remarkably deficient, there being a flatness, or rather a depression in the site of the organ. I took a cast of her forehead, a copy of which is in the museum of the Edinburgh Phrenological Society.

144 LANGUAGE.

organ, than in relation to any other. In judging of musical talent, unless great attention is paid to the training which the organ has received, error is very apt to be committed. Temperament, also, has a most important effect; and it ought not to be forgotten, that many persons sing and perform respectably, from little else than Imitation and practice.

33. LANGUAGE.

What external sign indicates a good endowment of Language?

Prominence of the eyes, or their depression vertically. This arises from the position of the organ on the posterior and transverse part of the upper orbitary plate,[92] immediately over the eye. When the organ is large, this plate is necessarily lower than in other cases, and the eyes are thus pushed forward and downward. In the sketch here given of Van Swieten's head, we have a good idea of a large development of Language.

[92] The orbitary plates are portions of the frontal bone, from which they go off backwards at right angles, forming a roof to the eye, and supporting the anterior lobes of the brain.

What talent depends on this organ?

That of verbal memory. The person has a great knack at recollecting words: he acquires languages with facility, learns readily by heart, and is generally a great talker. When Imitation is large, the power of pronouncing a foreign tongue after the manner of the natives is greatly increased. When small, the individual may easily acquire the language, and speak it with grammatical accuracy, but his pronunciation will be defective. Some people who have an admirable talent for acquiring languages, can never pronounce them well, owing to feebleness in the imitative faculty.

May a person be eminent as a linguist, and yet not remarkable for the prominency of his eyes?

He may; and hence mistakes are now and then committed by the inexperienced. If the organs of Locality, Weight, Size, Colouring, and Order, be very large, and the eyebrows full and overhanging, the eyes will appear much less prominent than in other circumstances.

Do prominent eyes always indicate talkativeness or verbal memory?

Always, except when the prominency is occasioned by fat, as is sometimes the case with corpulent people, especially if they be of dissipated habits. These, however, are merely exceptions to a well established general rule.

Why do very ordinary men often surpass at school, those who prove much their superiors in after life?

This generally arises from their possessing a good development of Language, Individuality, and Eventuality, especially the first. Men of great talent are often only moderately endowed with Language, while people, otherwise common-place, have frequently the faculty in great perfection. " When the doctrines of Phrenology come to be generally understood, the admiration excited by the possession of a great number of dead and foreign languages will be much diminished. It will then be considered merely as evidence of a large organ of Language, and as no evidence of superior general talents."[94]

What happens when the organ is large?

The person is a formidable linguist, or most insufferable talker, perhaps both. People of this sort have an absolute pleasure in hearing themselves speak. They are, literally, talking-machines, and are rendered uncomfortable if not allowed to indulge in their favourite occupation. Their style of writing and speaking is apt to be diffuse, and destitute of condensation : they can scribble whole pages, and talk by the hour, about absolutely nothing.

What results from a small development?

Difficulty in acquiring languages; hence indifferent scholarship; a want of facility in expression, and a disposition to be taciturn. The writings of such persons contain hardly a useless word, so that they are often more valuable and interesting than the works of the other class.

Mention a few eminent persons in whom the organ was large?

Swift, Haller, Leibnitz, Cobbett, and Edmund Burke. It appears large in the likenesses of Milton, who was a distinguished scholar, and a great master in his native language —witness " Paradise Lost," which, as a piece of mere verbal composition, and without reference to the sublimity of its ideas, is, perhaps, the most perfect work of modern times.

Is the organ of Language ever unnaturally excited?

In fever, mania, and drunkenness, this sometimes happens; the consequence of which is an inordinate propensity to talk, although the person may be, at other times, very taciturn. There have been instances, where, from the ex-

[94] Silas Jones' Phrenology.

citement of the organ during the delirium of fever, a language learned in early life, but afterwards forgotten, has been recalled, so that the person could speak it fluently, only, however, to be forgotten so soon as the excitement by which it had been resuscitated wore away. Cases where the memory of Languages is lost, from disease of this organ, are numerous.[95]

GENUS III.—REFLECTIVE FACULTIES.

What is the nature of the Reflective faculties ?

To produce the quality of reasoning or reflection. They compare one thing with another, and trace the relation subsisting between effects and their causes.

34. COMPARISON.

Where is this organ situated?

In the centre of the upper region of the forehead, immediately above Eventuality.

What is the nature of its faculty?

It enables us to trace resemblances and perceive analogies. Homer compares the eloquence of Ulysses to the soft falling of the snow flakes, and naturalists speak of the analogy

---

[95] I know a case of this kind. A literary gentlemen was actively employed for some months in the compilation of a French and English dictionary. He performed his laborious task, but, at the end of it, so completely had his organ of Language been overworked by its long continued exertions, that he actually lost the memory of words. His knowledge of Greek, Latin, and French, which was very extensive, vanished from his mind, nor did he recover it till the energy of the exhausted organ was restored to its wonted power, by being allowed to rest. Some years ago, when labouring under a fever, accompanied with violent cerebral action, I lost, for some days, to a considerable extent, the memory of words, although in all other respects, the mind was perfectly sound. If I wished a draught of water, I knew the thing wanted, but could not name it.

subsisting between the animal and vegetable kingdoms. It is the organ in question which associates these objects or qualities together, and traces similitude between them. Persons in whom it is large will trace a resemblance or affinity between objects or events which would entirely elude the observation of others with a smaller endowment. It is the well from which gushes forth figurative language; the grand fountain of similes, metaphors, and analogies. John Bunyan likens the christian's progress to that of a traveller in a dangerous country; death he represents as like the passage over a river from one country to another. In the scriptures, Christ is compared to the brazen serpent which Moses lifted up, and which was a remedy to the Israelites for the wounds inflicted by serpents. The universities have been compared to beacons moored in the stream of time, which serve only to mark the rapidity with which the tide of improvement flows past them. An author who arrives at the end of a dry dissertation, of which he is heartily tired, and is about to commence the discussion of an agreeable subject, likens himself to a traveller who has long toiled through a barren and disgusting track, and at length, after much labour, has reached the summit of an eminence from which he looks back on the country where his toils were endured, and sees before him with gladness the inviting territory now to be traversed. The life of a wicked man flows like a polluted stream. A beautiful woman without virtue is like a painted sepulchre. As iron sharpeneth iron, so is the face of a man to his friend. The people which sat in darkness saw a great light. Frail man! his days are like the grass. The kingdom of heaven is like a mustard seed. All the foregoing similitudes and analogies are the result of Comparison.

Does this faculty take cognizance of all kinds of comparisons?

No. Each intellectual faculty compares in matters strictly relating to itself. Thus, Form compares forms, Colouring colours, Size magnitudes, Tune the modulations of sound, &c. When Milton speaks of Satan standing "like Teneriffe or Atlas unremoved," or likens his shield to the full moon, it is Form that suggests the resemblance, and not Comparison. The province of the latter is to perceive analogies between objects falling under the cognizance of two different faculties, between ideas in themselves essentially different. When Coleridge, for instance, addresses Mont Blanc as a kingly spirit throned among the hills, he does so under the influence of the present faculty. If we hear music, it is Tune which compares the different notes and judges of their harmony or discord; but if we contrast together tunes and colours, if we say that the sober livery of Autumn is like a strain of plaintive music, it is then the faculty of Comparison which is brought into play.

Does the organ determine the nature of the similes which we employ?

No. This depends upon our other faculties. Thus, a person whose Tune is very powerful will draw similitudes from music; another, with ample Colouring, will deduce them from the hues of nature, &c.; a third, with Constructiveness well developed, may have recourse to comparisons from the steam engine. The present organ, therefore, although it gives the talent and the aptitude for indulging in similes, metaphors, and analogies, gives no farther. The character of these is determined by other powers.

In what class of people may we expect to find the organ large?

In popular poets, orators, preachers, and philosophical writers. In them the faculty is highly useful, from the abundant supply of imagery, and the wide and varied range of illustration which it affords. It appears large in Kant, Pitt, and

Dr. Chalmers, and remarkably in Mr. Thomas Moore, whose prolific power of comparison, as displayed in "Lalla Rookh," "The Loves of the Angels," and other poems, is unsurpassed, or rather unequalled. Roscoe, Henry IV. Goethe, Burke, and Curran, show a large development. The same remark applies to La Fontaine, the celebrated fabulist; and, according to Dr. Gall, children in whom the comparative faculty is strong, prefer fables to every other kind of instruction. The organ is better developed in some nations than in others. It is generally large in the Hindoo head, and the figurative character of the language of that people has long been proverbial.[96]

Kant.

[96] In a gentleman whose case is related in the 36th number of the Phrenological Journal, the activity of Comparison is so strong, that it prompts him

35. CAUSALITY.

Describe the position and function of this organ?

It lies in the forehead, on each side of Comparison, and the purpose served by it is to give the idea of connexion between cause and effect. He who is well endowed with it and Comparison, possesses a severe and logical intellect: he traces results from their origin, and is a sound reasoner. Men of this stamp are never shallow; they constitute the profound thinkers so rarely to be met with in society.

Is this a valuable faculty?

With the exception of Conscientiousness, it is, perhaps, the most valuable of the whole series. It is the faculty on which mainly depends the intellectual greatness of Locke, Bacon, Gall, and other illustrious names. The organ was

to compare names with physical objects:—Thus, the words Combe, Cox, and Simpson, resemble the following figures:—

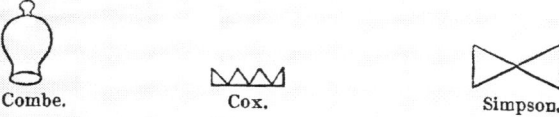

Combe. Cox. Simpson.

He has also an irresistible tendency to compare sounds with colour. When a musical instrument is played, one tone seems to him to resemble blue, another green, another purple, and so on. When this individual was attending Dr. Gall's lectures in Paris, some years ago, the Doctor was so struck with the appearance of the organ of Comparison in his forehead, that he pointed it out to his class, as an instance of great development, having, at the moment, no knowledge whatever of the person, or the degree in which he was endowed with the comparative faculty. I know a gentleman who has the same tendency to compare sounds and colours, and these are the only two I have ever met with. A case is related of a blind boy, who, on being asked what like the colour of scarlet was, replied, that it resembled the sound of a trumpet. In this instance, it is possible that the association of ideas may have arisen from the boy being informed that soldiers wore scarlet coats, and that the trumpet was employed to call them together.

very large in the heads of these great men. Kant, Dr. Thomas Brown, Fichte, Mendelsohn, and indeed, all men of eminently philosophical minds, exhibit an ample development of it. The frontispiece is an accurate likeness of the great founder of the phrenological system, in whose mind the faculty under consideration was a predominating feature. The forehead is finely developed, Language, Imitation, Causality, Comparison, and Benevolence are very conspicuous. It is the head of a man of high intellect, much decision of purpose, and great nobleness of disposition.

To what pursuits does the organ in question lead?

To abstract philosophical studies in general. A strong love of logic and metaphysics is one of its tendencies; indeed, no person can be great as a reasoner without it.

Is it necessary in the physical sciences?

As necessary there as in the moral. Individuality gives us cognizance of existences, and Eventuality of occurrences, but it is Causality, joined with Comparison, which enables us to reason upon them, and turn them to proper use. The organ is large in the heads of Playfair, Cuvier, Guy Lussac, and other eminent natural philosophers. Great reflecting intellect, however, does not seem to be necessary for mathematical excellence.[97]

Is Causality necessary for historical writing?

Eminently so. Without this faculty, history would be a mere series of details, without dependence or connexion. The springs which moved the different personages, and promoted the different events, would never be investigated, and the whole work would present a series of effects without

---

[97] It is a common notion that mathematics strengthens the reasoning powers. The erroneousness of this opinion is very successfully characterized by Mr. Combe. See the fourth edition of his System of Phrenology, vol. ii. p. 503. The reflecting intellect of some distinguished mathematicians has been by no means remarkable. *Ex. Gr.* Sir John Leslie.

any suitable causes. The works of all great historians, such as Gibbon, Hume, Robertson, display a rich vein of Causality; nor can it be doubted, that in the heads of these eminent men the organ was amply developed.

Is it necessary for poetry?

No; but poetry is vastly improved by the interfusion of a philosophic spirit derived from Causality. The faculty reigned in the sublime intellects of Milton and Shakspeare, and prevails every where through their mighty works. There is a great deal of Causality in the writings of Pope, Dryden, and Wordsworth: it gives a philosophic hue to poetry, without impairing its imaginative character.

Does a person with distinguished reasoning powers always appear great in general society?

No. Men with good perceptive, or knowing organs, often appear to much greater advantage than those with the higher powers of mind conferred by eminent reflective faculties. A shallow, smart person, would be thought far more highly of by the bulk of mankind, than a Kant, a Bacon, or a Spurzheim. Brilliant men are not often profound: the circumstance, indeed, of a person appearing very great in a miscellaneous company, may generally be taken as an evidence that his reflective faculties are not of a very high order.

What is the cause of this?

The reflective faculties of men, in general, are not strong, and they can neither appreciate nor comprehend profound reasoning. Good perceptive organs being more common, their manifestations are easily understood, and better relished; whence quick, but shallow men, strike the common mind more forcibly than deep thinkers; and are more likely to succeed in the common affairs of life.[98]

---

[98] Great intellects require great occasions to appear advantageously. A smart, superficial, talkative, polite man, with a fund of anecdote, much plausibility, and of a money-making turn, may prove more successful as a

What happens when Causality is small?

In this case the arguments of such persons are illogical and inconsecutive. They experience great difficulty in tracing effects from their causes, and are incapable of any thing like deep and connected reasoning. From their feeble appreciation of the force of evidence, it is extremely difficult to convince such persons of the truth of Phrenology.

What are the abuses of Causality?

An excessive tendency to metaphysical speculations, to the neglect of the practical pursuits of life. Kant seems an instance of the abuse of this faculty. He is very often profound, but speculative and abstract, and often unintelligible. In his head, the reflective organs greatly predominate over all others. Causality, however, is far less likely to be abused than any other faculty, if we except Benevolence and Conscientiousness.

Has Causality any influence on the formation of religious belief?

A very important influence, not inferior, perhaps, to that

---

tradesman, than one whose intellectual calibre is of a far higher grade. Supposing Shakspeare, Locke, and Newton, to be associated together as linen-drapers, it is very evident that the firm would soon become bankrupt. Not one half of the faculties of the partners finding occupation in this business, they would be irresistibly led to direct them into some channel where they would meet with the requisite exercise. Instead of serving customers, and keeping a sharp look out upon expenditure and receipts, each member of the concern would be occupied in such a manner as to ensure its speedy ruin. We may conceive Shakspeare, while presiding over the ledger, taking a flight to the court of Macbeth, or fleeting with Ariel or Titania upon the clouds; Locke, while purchasing goods, sadly perplexed with the doctrine of innate ideas; and Newton, in the act of measuring off a yard of linen, absorbed in calculating the dimensions of a planet. The business, in short, would straightway go to wreck, and the illustrious trio of would-be-drapers figuring in the Gazette. The predominating faculties always demand gratification, and it is wrong to bring up a man of great powers of mind to any pursuit which does not permit of their being safely indulged. Many men of superior talent make bad shop-keepers, who would have excelled as physicians, barristers, or divines—these professions giving ampler scope to the higher faculties of the mind than a mere trade.

of Veneration and Wonder. Causality, enlightened by knowledge, leads mankind to infer a presiding First Cause, from the marks of wisdom and design which every where present themselves in the material universe. Veneration prompts to revere the Being whose existence is thus inferred: while Wonder is the source of that astonishment and admiration with which we contemplate His existence and attributes.

THE TEMPERAMENTS.

What is meant by the temperaments?

The temperaments are certain states of constitution which are found to have a great effect on the energy and activity of the brain, and system in general.

How are the temperaments classified?

The pure temperaments are four in number, the Lymphatic, the Sanguine, the Bilious, and the Nervous, but they are often found in combination; thus we have the Sanguine-Lymphatic, the Nervous-Bilious, the Bilious-Nervous, the Nervous-Sanguine, &c. Sometimes even three temperaments are united, and then we have the Nervous-Sanguine-Bilious, the Nervous-Sanguine-Lymphatic, and so on.[99]

What are the characteristics of the pure temperaments?

In the Lymphatic, the body is full, the flesh soft and flabby, the hair and complexion pale, the eyes expressionless, the pulse slow, and the person indolent, inanimate, loutish, and insipid. In the Sanguine, the hair is red or of a light chesnut tinge, the countenance florid, the eyes blue and sparkling, the muscles large and tolerably firm, and the spirits lively and boisterous. The Bilious is characterized by dark hair and coarse skin. The muscles are less than in the Sanguine, but harder, and there is little fat. Altogether, this temperament possesses much energy, and is the best for sustaining the system under great and long protracted

---

[99] We place the name of the predominating temperament first. For instance, the Nervous-Bilious implies that the former preponderates, and the Bilious-Nervous the reverse. We often say, that a person is 60 Bilious, and 40 Nervous, or 80 Sanguine, and 20 Lymphatic, &c., to give some idea of the proportions which he possesses of each temperament.

efforts.[100] The Nervous temperament is distinguished by fine silky hair, pale complexion, small muscles, sharp features, and often delicate health. It is the most excitable and sensitive of all the temperaments; but its efforts, though rapid and vivacious, are soon exhausted.[101]

What is the character of the mixed temperaments?

This depends upon that of the pure ones out of which they are formed; thus the Nervous-Bilious combines in

---

[100] This temperament is improperly named. There is no connexion whatever between it and an excess of bile, as might be inferred from its denomination, and as was ignorantly supposed by the ancients. The term Fibrous more distinctly indicates its character, and by this name it ought to be known.

[101] "Who," says Cobbett, in the third letter of his 'Advice to Young Men,' is to tell whether a girl will make an industrious woman? How is the purblind lover, especially, to be able to ascertain whether she whose smiles, and dimples, and bewitching lips, have half bereft him of his senses; how is he to be able to judge, from any thing that he can see, whether the beloved object will be industrious or lazy? Why, it is very difficult." "There are, however, certain outward signs, which, if attended to with care, will serve as pretty sure guides. And first, if you find the tongue lazy, you may be nearly certain the hands and feet are the same. By laziness of the tongue, I do not mean silence; I do not mean an absence of talk, for that, in most cases, is very good; but I mean a slow and soft utterance; a sort of sighing out of the words, instead of speaking them; a sort of letting the sounds fall out as if the party were sick at stomach. The pronunciation of an industrious person is generally quick and distinct, and the voice, if not strong, firm at least. Not masculine; as feminine as possible: not a croak nor a bawl, but a quick, distinct, and sound voice." "Look a little also at the labours of the teeth, for those correspond with the other members of the body, and with the operations of the mind."— "Get to see her at work upon a mutton chop, or a bit of bread and cheese, and if she deal quickly with these, you have a pretty good security for that activity, that stirring industry, without which a wife is a burden instead of a help." "Another mark of industry is a quick step, and a somewhat heavy tread, showing that the foot comes down with a hearty good will." "I do not like, and I never liked, your sauntering, soft-stepping girls, who move as if they were perfectly indifferent to the result."

The above is an excellent illustration of the difference between the Lymphatic and the more active temperaments. It is sketched by the hand of a master, and truth has guided every stroke of the pencil.

itself the qualities of the Nervous and the Bilious, and so of the others.

What temperament is most likely to be found in combination with each other?

Those which most clearly resemble each other are the most likely to be united: hence the Lymphatic and Sanguine, and the Nervous and Bilious often go together. Sometimes, however, we find the most dissimilar in combination.

The state of the brain, then, is influenced by the prevailing temperament?

So much so, that in inferring character, the temperament requires always to be taken into consideration. Supposing a lymphatic person to possess the same size and shape of brain as a bilious one, he will manifest far less energy and activity of mind.

What does this arise from?

The brain, in common with the rest of the body, partakes of the functional energy or inactivity communicated by the temperament. In the Lymphatic, for instance, the blood being sent with little energy to the brain, that viscus is naturally torpid in its actions. In the Sanguine and the Bilious, the reverse is the case: the pulse is stronger and quicker, a proof of the greater activity of the circulating system; and hence the brain is more vigorously stimulated, receiving from this smart passage of the blood through it superior activity and power of function.

Does the torpor of the Lymphatic temperament depend solely on inactivity of circulation?

It is considered that it may also, in a great measure, arise from the blood being of a more watery description than in the other varieties. At least, it is well known, that in the Lymphatic there is a great predominance of the glandular system, and of the aqueous secretions.

Does quality of brain correspond with the excellence of the temperament?

There is reason to suppose that it does. The texture of the cerebral system is conjectured to be very fine in the Nervous temperament, and the reverse in the Lymphatic.[102]

Does dissection demonstrate this?

In all likelihood it would do so, although the subject has not yet been sufficiently attended to by anatomists to enable us to speak decidedly. This much is certain, that the texture of the skull is influenced by the prevailing temperament, being fine and compact in the Nervous, coarse and open-grained in the Lymphatic. Moreover, the muscles are firm in the former, and flabby in the latter.

Do particular temperaments prevail more in some nations than in others?

Yes. The Lymphatic predominates greatly among the Dutch, and to a considerable degree among the Germans. The prevailing temperament in France is the Nervous, or, perhaps, the Nervous-Bilious. The Sanguine seems to prevail among the Swedes and Norwegians, and, combined with the Nervous, among the Irish.

What is the temperament of genius?

The Nervous and Bilious, or a mixture of them, are in a

---

[102] "Long-continued observation has led us to consider it as a general rule, that one inherent quality characterizes the various organs composing an individual human body; in other words, that if the bones be dense and firm, and the muscles compact and vivacious, the other organs of the body partake of the excellent quality, and the brain, among the rest, is capable of vigorous action. When the expression of the countenance is animated and refined, an active and vivacious brain is seldom, if ever, wanting."—*Phrenological Journal*, vol. viii. p. 595.—(We see the influence of temperament on the lower animals. The bones of the racer are much more compact than those of the draught horse, the muscles are also firmer and tougher, and the animal possesses that mingled vivacity and capability for continued exertion, which exist in persons well endowed with the Bilious and the Nervous temperaments. In sluggish animals, such as the cow, the hog, &c., Lymphatic very decidedly predominates.)

particular manner the temperaments of genius. Great genius, however, may accompany the Sanguine temperament. Such is the case with Professor Wilson. It is difficult to conceive a purely lymphatic person of distinguished genius.

Give illustrations of some of the temperaments.

The temperament of Pope, Voltaire, Keats, Kirke White, and Cowper, was evidently pure Nervous—that of Milton probably a mixture of the Nervous and Bilious—that of Shakspeare and Raphael, of the Nervous and Sanguine—and that of Julius Cæsar, Oliver Cromwell, and Wellington, of the pure Bilious. Alcibiades and Achilles seem to have been illustrations of the pure Sanguine, and Benjamin Franklin of the Sanguine-Bilious. The temperament of Gall was Bilious-Nervous, that of Spurzheim Nervous-Sanguine-Lymphatic. These facts we infer from what we know of the individuals by their actions and writings, and by their portraits, where these exist.

Have mental exertion and age any modifying influence on temperament?

They have. Great exercise of the brain has a tendency to eradicate the Lymphatic to a considerable extent. Such was the case with Dr. Spurzheim. By incessant intellectual labour he rendered himself much less lymphatic than he originally was, and never got very stout, although his natural tendency was towards *embonpoint*. His sisters, on the other hand, who possessed brains very inferior to his, and who never exerted them, became excessively corpulent and indolent. In Spurzheim, the great size of brain, combined with a considerable portion of the Nervous, and some degree of the Sanguine temperament, kept him intellectually very active, and contributed to mitigate the lymphatic influence. Age, again, has a tendency to induce the latter. People who showed little or none of it when young, often exhibit it when they get towards middle or advanced life, becoming then full-bodied and indolent, and indisposed to either corporeal or mental exertion.[103]

Does not this doctrine of the temperaments throw great obstacles in the way of predicating character?

It does not; for a knowledge of quality of brain is as much one of the phrenological conditions, as that of quantity. A true phrenologist always calculates the effect which temperament produces, seeing that on this the quality of the cerebral texture seems chiefly to depend. In estimating the strength of two men, we do not judge absolutely by their size: the one who is least in dimensions, may yet possess the greatest energy in his muscular system. If, however, the muscles of the large man are not only bulkier, but of equal quality as respects firmness and stamina, he must needs be the more athletic of the two. Other things being equal, the larger the muscles or brain, the greater will be the power possessed by them. A large lymphatic brain will display more vigour than a small one, although less than that of a brain acted on by more energetic temperaments.

[103] " We have heard it remarked by an acute traveller, that the Lymphatic temperament, indicated by coarse fair hair, plump and inexpressive countenance, and languid eyes, with the attendant dulness and coarseness of mind, greatly predominates among the lower orders in the northern countries of Europe; while dark hair and dark eyes, or fine flaxen hair, and clear vivacious blue eyes, indicative of the Bilious and Nervous temperaments, are much more common among the higher classes in the same regions; and that the proportions of the Bilious and Nervous temperaments to the Lymphatic, increase as the degrees of latitude decrease."—*Phrenological Journal*, vol. vii. p. 412.

MISCELLANEOUS QUESTIONS.

What faculties first display themselves?

The propensities, with one exception—that of Amativeness, which is the organ that last manifests the faculty belonging to it.

Do the Perceptive or the Reflective organs act earliest?

The perceptive: children soon begin to notice objects, but a long time elapses before they can reason upon them, or trace their relations.[104]

Are the organs generally contiguous whose functions bear some resemblance?

They are. Thus Causality and Comparison, which have a strong analogy in their functions, are contiguous. The same is the case with Ideality and Wonder, with Time and Tune, with Combativeness and Destructiveness, with Adhesiveness and Philoprogenitiveness, and so on. This curious

---

[104] " The reflecting faculties, observes Dr. Caldwell, "are never powerfully manifested at a very early period of life. The knowing or perceptive ones alone are, at times, inordinately vigorous in infancy. Hence, none of the precocious geniuses that appear excite astonishment by their reasoning powers. They are distinguished in music, numbers, drawing, painting, modelling, and language; but not in any thing that depends on depth of reflection; such as general philosophy, political economy, or abstract metaphysics. In these latter branches of science precocious geniuses rarely attain eminence at any period of their lives. Nature would seem to have so exhausted her resources in giving unwarranted luxuriance in them to the knowing organs of the brain, as to have but little left to bestow on the reflecting ones which come to maturity at a later period. Hence, it has passed almost into a proverb that 'early geniuses who are men among boys are apt to be afterwards boys among men.' Infant Rosciuses are mere mimics and verbalists, their organs of Imitativeness and Language being inordinately developed; and they seldom go beyond mimicry during their lives. We recollect no instance of an *infant* Roscius becoming an *adult* one."—*Annals of Phrenology*, vol. i. p. 61.

collocation of parts bearing a functional resemblance, is a strong presumptive evidence in confirmation of phrenology.

Are the faculties always affected in the same manner?

They are not. They may be affected painfully or the reverse according to circumstances. If I see a generous action performed, my Benevolence, supposing it to be full, is agreeably excited, and gratification is the result: an act of cruelty, on the other hand, affects it painfully, and produces a disagreeable feeling. Conscientiousness is gratified by honesty, and shocked by knavery; Adhesiveness is delighted in the society of a beloved friend, and pained by his absence or death. Acquisitiveness receives gratification from wealth, and is hurt by its loss. Objects of beauty please Ideality; squalid, filthy, disgusting objects pain it. The faculties, therefore, may be affected in two ways. Their agreeable affection constitutes pleasing; their disagreeable, painful emotions of the mind.

Is the exercise of any of the faculties pernicious?

This depends upon whether the degree in which they are exercised amounts to an abuse. All the faculties are in themselves good, if legitimately employed. The Creator endowed us with the whole of them that they might be rationally gratified; and any man who affirms that even a single one ought to be utterly stifled or blotted out, as it were, from the human mind is, in reality, offering an insult to the Divine Being by whom that mind was created. Some well-meaning, but unenlightened persons, imagine that such innocent occupations as dancing, music, mirth, and theatrical representations are offensive in the eyes of God. Now what is the tendency of this allegation, but to charge the Almighty with creating a number of useless or improper faculties? We have organs of Tune and Time, which inspire the love of music and dancing, and induce us to visit concerts and balls. We have an organ of Wit whose function is to give rise to mirthfulness. We have one of Ideality, which communicates poetic rapture, and experiences gratification in the magnificent performances of a Siddons, a Talma, or a Kean. If we do not allow the passion for these amusements to go to excess : if we indulge it moderately, avoiding abuse of the faculties from whence it springs, we are not only not doing what is morally wrong, but we are doing what is positively right, in so far as we thus obey a rational and beneficial impulse implanted in our minds by the author of nature, and wisely intended for our good. Dancing, music, poetry, and theatrical representations of a moral character, when had recourse to in the intervals of more urgent and laborious pursuits, have an excellent effect on the brain. They innocently and agreeably stimulate the different organs, especially those of the Sentiments and Intellect, and their tendency, instead of being pernicious, is highly favourable to virtue. What would be thought of the sanity of that man who proposed that the eyes should be perpetually blindfolded, and the ears stuffed with cotton, because we may misemploy the former in wilfully witnessing scenes of cruelty, or the latter in listening to obscene songs or profligate conversation. Those who proscribe the legitimate gratification of any of the faculties are acting a part equally foolish.

What is the cause of mental precocity?

It has its origin in premature development or excitement of the intellectual organs. The source of such prematurity, however, is rather obscure, but it seems to be connected in general with a high Nervous Temperament. Lymphatic or Bilious children are seldom precocious. Precocity is peculiarly common among the scrofulous, rickety, [105] and

---

[105] An American physician, Dr. Brigham, has published a little work entitled "Remarks on the influence of Mental Cultivation and Mental

consumptive. These states of constitution are accompanied with an irritable state of frame, which extends its influence to the brain, and thus causes a premature manifestation of its functions.

Why do precocious children generally turn out very ordinary as adults?

It is a law of nature, that when an organ is vehemently exercised, before acquiring full consistency and strength, its functions become impaired. A horse sent to the turf very young has its constitution often ruined, and the same is the case with youthful prize-fighters and recruits. The brain is no exception to the general rule.

Ought the mind of a child who exhibits marks of early genius, to be much exercised?

Quite the reverse. We ought to consider the brain of such a child as in a state of unnatural excitement bordering on disease; and if it be fond of thinking or studying much, the habit ought rather to be checked than encouraged. If we work the brain much, it is ten to one that it gets diseased, and the child is either cut off early, or lives to be, for ever after, a very common-place person, perhaps a blockhead. Hydrocephalus, or water in the head, is sometimes produced in children by over-exertion of the brain.

Does the same rule apply to dull children?

Not so powerfully. The minds of these children ought to be exercised, so as to give health to, and stimulate the brain; they need the spur instead of the bridle. Even here, however, there is a limit which it is dangerous to transgress. The brain of no child whatever ought to be much worked; moderate exercise is all that should be attempted. Very

Excitement on Health," which throws a flood of light upon this important subject. It has been reprinted, with many additional notes, by Messrs. Reid & Co. Booksellers in Glasgow, and ought to be read by every parent and teacher of youth.

great evils result from school education being too severe and too early begun.

How happens it that dull children often prove very clever as adults?

From the fact, that in some individuals the intellectual organs are slow of reaching maturity, either from late growth or late excitement. Some minds are very late of being evolved. Gessner the Swiss Poet was, at the age of ten years, declared by his preceptors incapable of any attainment; and Swift, Thomson, Sir Walter Scott, and Dr. Johnson, were very dull lads. Massillon, Byron, Gibbon, and Voltaire, exhibited in boyhood and youth no indications of more than ordinary talent; while Sir Isaac Newton, according to his own account, ranked very low in the school till the age of twelve, when his superior powers began to develop themselves. Persons in whom the reflective organs predominate over the perceptive, are more likely to be considered dull in youth, than when there is an opposite configuration of brain; the former reflective organs, as already mentioned, being longer of attaining maturity of action than the others.

From what parent do children chiefly derive their qualities?

In colour and form, the father, if these are in him very strong, transmits a greater share of his qualities, apparently because he is frequently before the mother, and thus impresses her strongly with the idea of them; but in giving temperament and shape of brain, the mother's influence seems to be the greatest. Hence a clever woman and an ordinary man, are more likely to have talented children than the converse. Men of genius generally marry dull women—hence their children are often dull.[106] Another

---

[106] If both parents are talented, there is every chance of the children being so. The union of Godwin and Mary Wolstoncroft, produced Mrs.

reason is, that such men frequently infringe the organic laws, by overworking their brains, and not studying the rules of health sufficiently: defective brains are in this way transmitted to their children.[107]

Why are the first-born of parents who marry very young, generally inferior in intellect and morality to those that come afterwards?

Parents communicate their qualities of brain to offspring. In young parents, the activity of the propensities is greater, and that of the intellect and moral sentiments less than at a later period. A child produced at a time when the cerebral system of its father and mother is in this immature state, partakes of the defect, and retains it through life.[108] Those produced, when the intellect and moral feelings are brought into more vigorous operation, naturally enjoy the

---

Shelley, the distinguished author of Frankenstein; and other examples might be adduced.

Vice is propagable from parents to their children, in the same way as virtue and talent. Henry II. of France and his Queen, Catherine de Medicis, were cruel and atrocious bigots. The former, on the coronation of his wife, burned many protestants alive, and regaled himself with the horrid spectacle. Catherine, who succeeded him as Regent, was not less infamous for her cruelty. From this abominable couple sprung three sons still more wicked than their parents,—viz. Francis II., Charles IX., and Henry III.; the second named being the author of the horrid massacre of St. Bartholomew's day, on which occasion 40,000 Protestants were butchered in cold blood.

[107] For much valuable information on the subject of the transmission of hereditary qualities from parents to their children, the reader is referred to Dr. Caldwell's admirable little work entitled "Thoughts on Physical Education," a reprint of which has lately appeared in Edinburgh under the auspices of Mr. Combe and Mr. Robert Cox, the former of whom has furnished it with a preface, and the latter with a variety of excellent notes. See also Mr. Combe's "Constitution of Man."

[108] I confess myself a participator in the vulgar belief that impressions made upon the mother's mind during pregnancy may affect the offspring. There are many cases to prove this. Mr. Bennet relates a very striking one in the "London Medical and Physical Journal." A woman gave birth

benefit of this improved condition of brain, and the probabilities are, that they will surpass the eldest born both in talents and in virtue.

What is the best plan for insuring a good brain to our offspring?

The first great point is obedience to the organic laws of marriage, which command us to choose for partners only such as have a good cerebral organization. The next is ample nourishment in childhood, with considerable bodily, and moderate mental exercise.

In which sex do the faculties soonest reach maturity?

In the female. Woman attains her full stature and proportions earlier than man; and the same law prevails also with regard to the manifestations of her mind.

Is mental maturity attained at the same age in all nations?

No. In the tropics this occurs several years earlier than in the colder regions.

Has the size of brain any effect upon the voice?

It has, especially if the organs of Firmness, Combative-

---

to a child with a large cluster of globular tumours growing from the tongue, and preventing the closure of the mouth, in colour, shape, and size exactly resembling our common grapes; and with a red excrescence from the chest as exactly resembling in figure and general appearance a turkey's wattles. On being questioned, before the child was shown her, she answered that, while pregnant, she had seen some grapes, longed intensely for them and constantly thought of them, and once was attacked by a turkey cock. James VI. of Scotland had a great abhorrence of a drawn sword, and was, withal, timid and cowardly; which difference of character from that of all the line of Stewart which preceded and followed him has been attributed, not irrationally, to the circumstance of Rizzio having been butchered before the eyes of Queen Mary then *enceinte* with the future monarch. According to Esquirol, the children whose existence dated from the horrors of the first French Revolution turned out to be weak, nervous, and irritable in mind, extremely susceptible of impressions, and liable to be thrown, by the least extraordinary excitement, into absolute insanity. The story of Jacob and the rods, as related in the 30th chapter of Genesis, is a proof of the belief in ancient time that parental impressions may affect the offspring.

ness, and Destructiveness are large. Large-brained people have generally a loud, energetic pronunciation—small-brained the reverse.

Why are certain individuals much liked by some and hated by others?

Individuals with large organs of Benevolence, Self-Esteem, and Destructiveness, will be objects of love or aversion, according to the dispositions of those they associate with. If they come in contact with people who are also largely endowed with the two latter organs, they will probably be disliked, from the almost necessary collision of faculties which will ensue betwixt the parties. Meeting with persons in whom the organs in question are small, or only moderately developed, no such collision takes place; and their Benevolence, having uninterrupted sway, comes into operation, and attracts towards themselves the kindly feelings of those persons.

Why are brave people generally affectionate?

This arises from the curious fact, that when Combativeness is greatly developed, there is almost always a large organ of Adhesiveness. Accordingly, brave men have ever been remarked for the strength of their attachments. General Wurmser had both organs large, and he displayed the corresponding faculties powerfully. In the skull of king Robert Bruce, Adhesiveness is amply developed; and history represents him as an affectionate husband and friend.

Why are passionate people remarkable for their dislikes and attachments?

Such persons have in general exciteable temperaments, very active brains; and this activity applies to Destructiveness and Adhesiveness, in common with other organs. The excitement of the first named will produce irascibility and hatred, that of the latter affection and kindness.

Why does it sometimes happen that a servant who has

been under two mistresses is esteemed by one a person of excellent temper, and by the other quite the reverse?

This arises undoubtedly from the different constitutions of mind possessed by the two mistresses. If the servant is destructive and the mistress the same, the hasty temper of the former will probably often appear: if the mistress is of a mild disposition, the organ of Destructiveness in the servant will not be called into activity, and she will be regarded by her employer as possessed of a very good temper. This teaches us that, in selecting servants, care should be taken to procure those whose dispositions will accord with our own. By neglecting this obvious rule, quarrels are perpetually occurring, and a great deal of domestic annoyance is the result. It teaches, moreover, something still more important. If a man, for instance, with large Destructiveness, Combativeness and Firmness, marries a woman similarly organized, there is a great chance of unhappiness, unless the parties have the most admirable prudence and self-command. Common observation points out the consequences of such ill-assorted unions.

Has Phrenology been ever usefully employed in the selection of servants?

It has, and with such success that some phrenologists will not engage a servant without ascertaining his or her character by examination of the head. The practice is altogether excellent, and should be more generally had recourse to. A full development of Order, Individuality, and Conscientiousness is absolutely essential to a good domestic. Where children are to be taken care of, Philoprogenitiveness ought to be large, otherwise little interest will be felt in them. Veneration, which bestows deference to superiors, should also be well developed, especially if the master or mistress possesses much Self-Esteem. A servant with a small brain and feeble character may suit an employer similarly situated, but will not answer one whose brain is large and active. To the latter he will seem inefficient or useless. The servant, however, ought not to excel his master in intellect or force of character. If such is the case, he will intuitively feel that nature has made him superior to the master he serves. An active temperament is in every case essential. Where the lymphatic tendency prevails, smartness and vivacity will be absent, and work felt to be toilsome and oppressive. Because a servant is rejected by one master, on the score of inefficiency, it by no means follows that he may not make a very fair one to another, with a different cerebral combination.[109]

If a woman with a large active brain, marries a small-brained man, what is likely to ensue?

She will rule her husband. As already mentioned, a large brain acquires an ascendency over a small one.

Why, then, do weak women sometimes rule men superior to themselves in intellect and force of character?

Such men will often give way in trifling matters to their wives for the sake of peace, but not in affairs of real importance. A sensible man will not run the risk of quarrelling with a silly woman, when, by yielding in things of no great moment, he can keep her quiet. Independently of this, strong-minded men are often very much attached to their

---

[109] "In one instance, I refused to hire a boy as a servant, because I found his head to belong to the inferior class, although he was introduced by a woman whose good conduct and discrimination I had long known, and who gave him an excellent character. That individual was, at first, greatly incensed at my refusing to engage the boy; but within a month she returned, and said that she had been grossly imposed upon herself by a neighbour, whose son the boy was; that she had since learned that he was a thief, and had been dismissed from his previous service for stealing. On another occasion, I hired a female servant, because her head belonged to the superior class, although her former mistress gave her a very indifferent character; and the result was equally in favour of phrenology. She turned out an excellent servant, and remained with me for several years, until she was respectably married."—*Combe's System*, 4th edition, vol. ii. p. 717.

wives, however much inferior to themselves; and are naturally not indisposed to gratify their whimsicalities. When a man, intellectually superior to his wife, is ruled and overawed by her, it will be found that he is her inferior in the energy of the propensities. These, when strong and active, give force to the character, and a natural predominance to the individual over others more highly gifted with intellect, but with the propensities feebler. Such, sometimes, is the secret of female sway over intellectually superior minds.

Why is parental generally stronger than filial love?

Because in the first case both Adhesiveness and Philoprogenitiveness come into operation, whereas in the second it is Adhesiveness alone that acts.

What does eccentricity arise from?

From a want of due balance in the faculties. If one organ or more is large in proportion to the others, particularly where the intellect is weak, it will produce that irregularity of character to which the term eccentric is applied. Eccentricity frequently degenerates into madness.

From what does a great flow of animal spirits proceed?

From unusual activity of brain, accompanied often with deficient prudence and reflection, and a large development of Hope, Ideality, and Wit. Such cerebral activity is constitutional, and generally accompanied with a high sanguineous temperament.

When an organ is much exercised, is pain ever felt in the site of it?

Very often. Hard-thinking produces a sense of fulness or pain in the forehead, the seat of the intellectual organs. In excitement of Amativeness, there is frequently a sense of heat at the nape of the neck. When there exists a strong desire to travel,[110] pain is sometimes felt in the region of

---

[110] "A young lady," says Dr. Gall, "had always a great desire to travel. She eloped from her father's house with an officer. Grief and remorse un-

Locality; and, in cases of spectral illusions, over the perceptive organs.

What is the cause of spectral illusions?

These phenomena depend on a morbidly excited state of some of the perceptive organs, such as Form, Size, and Colour; whence images are presented to the mind without the co-operation of the external senses. If the organ of Form, for instance, becomes as strongly stimulated by an internal cause as it would be by an object presented to it by the vision, some image will be formed, and the person will believe that he sees what in reality has no existence. Morbid affections of the nerves of sight seem to have the same influence in producing spectral illusions.

Is the feeling of hunger experienced, strictly speaking, in the stomach?

No. The term "craving of the stomach," so often used to express hunger, is not in reality correct. The brain is the craver, and is excited to a craving state only by emptiness of the stomach, unless the organ of Alimentiveness be so large, or so stimulated by some internal morbid action, as to need no such excitement; or unless disease be present in the stomach, so as to transmit to the brain the sensation which, during health, is transmitted during inanition alone.

dermined her health. I attended her, and she made me remark two large prominences which, she said, the pain she had endured had caused to grow on her forehead. These excrescences, which appeared to her the consequences of divine wrath, were in fact the organs of Locality, to which she had never paid any attention." To this I may add, that a lady of my acquaintance, in whom the organ of Philoprogenitiveness is very largely developed even for a woman, and whose love of children is extreme, informs me that when distressed or anxious about her family she experiences pain at the back of the head, just over the seat of the organ. Some deny the possibility of one part of a healthy brain being more gorged with blood than another. The above facts sufficiently demonstrate that such may be the case; nor can it be doubted that in a fit of violent rage, the portion of the cerebral mass which manifests Destructiveness is in a much more turgescent state than that appropriated to Benevolence.

People are sometimes afflicted with imaginary voices speaking to them: can you account for this?

It may be explained in the same way as apparitions. There are unquestionably certain parts of the brain which take cognizance of sounds: we call the nerve of the ear the organ of hearing, but strictly speaking it is not such: it is merely the medium for conveying sounds to the brain, where the true organ resides. Now, suppose that the portion of the brain appropriated to this sense is stimulated by some internal cause, in the same way as it is by real sounds conveyed to it by the nerve, the person will have the idea that he hears, and that often as distinctly as if subjected to the stimulus of actual noise. Fanatics and deranged people sometimes imagine they hear angels, and even the Deity, speaking to them; and persons perfectly deaf have at times sensations as of voices addressing them, just as the blind are occasionally haunted by spectral illusions. All these phenomena are explicable upon the principles just mentioned.[111]

What are dreams?

Dreams are merely spectral illusions—with this difference, that, in the former, only certain of the organs are vivified by the internal stimulus, while the rest are asleep; whereas, in the latter, all are in the usual waking state. When I see a ship sailing, in a dream, the organs of Form, Colouring, &c. are stimulated by some internal cause, just as they are in spectral illusions.

---

[111] Nothing is more common than spontaneous stimulation of the organ of Tune. We are then often haunted with what Matthews calls the ghost of a tune, which intrudes itself on all occasions, and sometimes under circumstances peculiarly ludicrous. I have heard of a worthy clergyman, who, while in the pulpit one Sunday, felt an excessive desire to sing Maggie Lauder; on going home the tendency to indulge in this profane freak became irresistible, and without more ado he went into his garden and sung the song with great glee. This done, the inclination vanished: his organ of Tune received the gratification for which it was craving, and the ghost of Maggie Lauder took to flight.

How does it happen that people of weak intellect sometimes display considerable powers of mind during an attack of fever or inflammation of the brain?

It is to be accounted for from the organs of the brain being stimulated by the disease; whence the faculties connected with these organs display unusual force, and an intellectual energy is exhibited of which, at other times, the person gives no indications. As soon, however, as the disease is removed, the stimulus communicated by it to the organs ceases, and the customary state of imbecility returns. Even idiots sometimes become rational during fever.

Explain why forgotten events are sometimes brought back to the mind in dreams.

This is explicable on the same principle. During the dream, certain portions of the brain which bear a relation to the event are stimulated, and a resuscitation of it is the consequence. A man, for instance, hides or mislays money, and forgets where; but the brain being excited, the circumstance is vividly recalled; and if he is ignorant, as generally happens, of the cause of this phenomenon, he straightway infers that something supernatural has occurred, and that he has been favoured with intelligence by spiritual agency.

Are all the cerebral organs liable to stimulation in madness, dreaming, drunkenness, &c.?

So far as we know, they all are; and there is no obvious reason why any of them should be exempted from this law.

Give a few instances of the stimulation of particular organs.

People who never displayed any talent for poetry, music, calculation, or eloquence, have exhibited these qualities in considerable perfection during an attack of insanity, or even in dreams: the most chaste have become wanton in their conduct, and indecent in their language;

the most sedate witty; the most prosaic full of imagination. Even persons who never before displayed any thing like logical power, have reasoned profoundly, constituting instances of what Pinel calls " Folie Raisonnante," or Reasoning Insanity. Such changes undoubtedly arise from the particular stimulus which has been communicated to the organs of the faculties concerned.

May a man be a ready, eloquent, and impressive speaker, and yet possess no great intellect?

Nothing is more common. It is generally but fallaciously imagined that eloquence is altogether an intellectual operation; and hence those who excel in it are looked upon as necessarily possessing very superior talents. Much of the power of eloquence, however, is derived from the appeals made by it to the propensities and sentiments. A person who addresses the passions of a multitude, and carries his audience along with him, is truly eloquent; and yet in accomplishing this oratorical feat, scarcely a single appeal may be made to the intellect of his hearers. The harangues of popular demagogues are almost all of this sort. They address the Self-Esteem, the Combativeness, and the Love of Approbation of the crowd, and the effect produced is often wonderful. The late Henry Hunt owed the power which he wielded of swaying a mob, to his strong propensities, finding a ready echo in those of his audience. In a war of the lower propensities he was a formidable gladiator; and so will any man be who is gifted with powerful passions, and a large organ of Language. The eloquence which appeals to the understanding alone, is indeed a very different and very superior accomplishment; but for common purposes it is little available, in so far as the average intellects of men are not sufficiently enlightened to relish it. This is the reason why some men of great talent are little appreciated as speakers by the multitude, while others, who appeal solely to the feelings of an audience, and whose intellectual calibre is exceedingly small, are looked upon as persons of distinguished genius.

How is it that people of talent have sometimes small, and dull people large heads?

To bestow talent, the intellectual organs only are necessary. A person may have these well developed, and yet the organs of the propensities and inferior sentiments may be so small, as to cause the head to be below the average size. Again, if the former class be small, and the latter very large, the head may be one of ample dimensions, and yet its owner be a most ordinary mortal. Where organs not remarkably developed accompany strong faculties, the mental cultivation will be found to have been great, and the quality of brain to be very superior.

In a person of talent, would you expect a large intellectual development?

I would, provided his talent was of a comprehensive kind; but it is quite possible to possess a genius for a particular subject, and yet have a poor general development of the intellectual organs. For instance, he may have great talent in calculation, in music, or in scholarship, by virtue of large organs of Number, Tune, or Language. People are often called clever, from possessing, in great perfection, one particular faculty; and, having what phrenologists would call a poor development of brain, they are brought forward as illustrations of the fallacy of the science. George III. was called by some people a clever man, because he possessed great power of recollecting individuals whom he had seen. There was once a man who could repeat, from memory, the whole of the New Testament. Many hearing of such a prodigy, would infer that he must have been possessed of vast genius; yet he was little better than an idiot.

Has a tall man a larger brain than one of moderate stature?

A sufficient number of observations appears still awanting to determine this point satisfactorily; but it seems probable, that the brain of a tall, broad, powerful man, is, generally speaking, larger than that of a short man of an opposite make. The heads, at all events, of these men are commonly larger; but this may partly arise from the skull and integuments being generally very thick in athletic subjects. Large men, however, are usually inferior in intellect and energy of character to the middle-sized, and are far less likely to possess the same amount of genius with the same size of brain—the nervous energy being wasted over their unwieldy trunks in the processes of digestion, assimilation, secretion, &c.[112] "Large men," as Richerand justly remarks, "are seldom great men."

Is great muscular exercise favourable to the vigorous action of the brain?

Quite the reverse. A hard-working man, after finishing his day's labour, will be apt to fall asleep if he attempts to read. In him, the nervous energy is chiefly expended on the muscles, and too small a portion of it is sent to the intellectual organs, which, not being stimulated sufficiently, are in a state unfavourable to the process of thinking. In a country church, nothing is more common than to find half the congregation asleep during sermon; and the reason is

---

[112] Though large men seem to have, generally speaking, larger brains than the middle-sized, the exceptions to this rule are numerous. Gall, Byron, Cuvier, and Napoleon, had very large heads, and none of them exceeded the ordinary size; the latter two, indeed, were rather below it. The same remark applies to Godwin, whose head was of great size. With regard to the fact of large bodies being unfavourable to mental activity and power, Spurzheim remarks, that "A large body will require the greater part of the brain and nervous system to be employed in its functions, and there will then remain a small portion for the manifestations of the superior faculties." I may here observe, that when the body is growing rapidly, the mind becomes weak, on account of the drafts made upon the brain, to effect the growth—in other words, to supply the nervous energy necessary for the proper performance of the digestive and assimilative functions.

obvious. Country people, working harder than citizens in general, have less vivacious brains. An intellectual effort overcomes them sooner, and they fall asleep, where the others would continue awake without difficulty.

In certain cases of insanity, there is said to be no apparent disease of the brain: how is this reconcileable with phrenology?

Although there is no apparent, there must be real disease. Facts prove that disease may exist without its being possible to ascertain it by dissection. Such is often the case in tetanus, tic doloureux, and paralysis, where we can generally detect no change whatever in the nerves, the seat of those diseases. In like manner, digestion, or the biliary secretion, may be disordered, without the concomitance of any appreciable change in the stomach or liver; and so may it be with the brain in what are called mental diseases. The cases of insanity, however, in which this viscus is seemingly free from disease, must be exceedingly few in number, if any such there be at all. One of the most distinguished of modern physiologists, Mr. Lawrence, states that he has examined the heads of many insane persons after death, and has hardly seen a single brain in which there were not obvious marks of disease. Dr. Wright of the Bethlehem Lunatic Asylum says, that in one hundred cases of insane individuals, whose heads he had examined, all exhibited signs of disease, more or less. A French writer, who has examined a still greater number, arrives at the same conclusion. In short, it is more than probable, that in every case, a skilful person, who is accustomed to examine the brains of lunatics, will detect signs of disease. They may be so slight as to escape the notice of a common observer, but that they will be manifest to the minute, experienced, and talented pathologist, there is every reason to believe.

MISCELLANEOUS QUESTIONS.

How happens it that in extensive dropsy of the brain, the intellectual powers are not always destroyed?

When hydrocephalus (or water in the head) occurs before the process of cranial ossification is perfected, or even at a later period, the bones yield to the action of the internal fluid, and the brain is thus, in a great measure, freed from a pressure which would otherwise speedily prove fatal. The size which the head then attains is often enormous. It is customary to

Illustration of Hydrocephalus.

say that in some such cases the intellect is not weakened, but this is a mistake. Destroyed it may not be, but impaired it always is, more or less. A hydrocephalic brain may exhibit tolerable aptitude where a very moderate demand is made upon its energies; but engage it in any task which requires considerable exertion, and its weakness and inefficiency will be abundantly evident.

What do you think of the objection often made to phrenology, that the organs cannot be shown in a detached state, but only homogeneously connected?[113]

Every sensible person must think it a very absurd one. If the purpose of Nature had been to settle the doubts of a few incredulous individuals, instead of constructing the brain after the fashion best adapted for the performance of its functions, then, doubtless, she would have marked the limits of every organ with mathematical nicety and distinctness; but it has not pleased her to do this—at least so far as our powers of observation at present enable us to discover; and, accordingly, we must just take things as we find them —satisfied, that the animal economy exhibits no instance of one organ performing more than one function, and that in assigning different functions to different parts of the brain, Nature is only following one of her own invariable laws.

Is not the tongue, though it possesses taste, sensation, and motion, three different functions, a single organ?

There are certainly three functions combined in the tongue,

---

[113] Let such objectors point out (as was suggested in a humorous paper in the Phrenological Journal) where the chin ends and the cheeks begin, and then we shall allow their arguments to possess some force. No human being can point out the line of demarcation which separates those parts of the face, yet, I presume, every man of sound mind admits the existence of chins, and the possibility of telling whether they are large or small. The organs of the brain are not a whit more intimately blended together, than is the chin, or even the nose, with the cheeks. In looking at a mountain, no person can tell the precise point where it commences, and the plain terminates; still, common sense informs us, that there is a mountain before our eyes. In looking at the rainbow, or through a prism, we see a variety of differently coloured rays, yet who can define the limits of each? Though perfectly distinct, they are blended together in a way that defies the pointing out of their limits. So it is with the organs of the brain.

it must be considered that each of these is effected by means of a distinct organ or nerve. We have a nerve for taste, another for sensation, and a third for motion—so that, strictly speaking, the tongue is not a single organ, but combines in itself several, by means of which its varied functions are performed. Its different nerves can perform only their own functions and no other; thus, in the gustatory nerve resides the sense of taste alone, and not that of feeling—just as, in the brain, the organ of Locality gives us the perception of places, and not that of music or colour. The fact, therefore, that one organ can perform only one function holds as true in the tongue as in the brain; and throughout the whole animal economy it is precisely the same.[114]

What is crime?

The abuse of certain of the propensities: thus, theft is the abuse of Acquisitiveness, and murder of Destructiveness. Crime, however, presupposes such a decree of sanity as to make us responsible agents, for no possible abuse of the propensities can be looked upon as criminal in a madman or an idiot.

What is the origin of motives?

Motives are desires or inclinations produced by the activity of the faculties; and this activity is owing to the excitement of the cerebral organs, either spontaneous, or the effect of

---

[114] Till the discovery of Sir Charles Bell, no person could anatomically demonstrate the existence of distinct nerves for motion and sensation. Spurzheim, judging from analogy, inferred, that there must be separate nerves for each of these functions, and urged anatomists to prosecute the subject, and endeavour to find them out. Sir Charles Bell was the lucky discoverer. He ascertained that the one set of nerves arises from the anterior, and the other from the posterior part of the spinal marrow, that they unite almost immediately, and are so intimately blended, that they cannot be distinguished or disentangled. They are, in fact, as completely incorporated, to all appearance, as the different organs of the brain, and constitute a texture seemingly even more homogeneous than the cerebral mass.

external circumstances, or, what is most frequent, arising from both.

Would every man have acted as the murderer Hare did, if placed in the same circumstances?

No. Few men could possibly have done so, and none unless they had possessed a cerebral organization similar to Hare's. No longing for money, no privation, however great, could have made thieves or murderers of such men as Fenelon and Howard.

What is the cause of certain organs being too large or too active?

This very often arises from infringement of the organic laws in marriage. If a man with great Combativeness and Destructiveness, marries a woman similarly endowed, their children will probably possess the preponderating organs still larger and more active than the parents. The activity of the propensities is often increased by drinking, and the contamination of bad society, for the same reason that the vigour of the reflecting faculties is augmented by reading, and other salutary intellectual exercises.

May deficiency in the size of certain organs be also occasioned by infringement of the organic laws?

Undoubtedly. A man and woman very deficient in Conscientiousness, will be apt to produce dishonest children. If both parents have a poor intellectual development, their offspring almost always inherit the same—in most cases to a worse degree.

Have the heads of criminals any peculiarity of formation?

They have, in so far that not an instance can be pointed out, of a criminal, or notoriously worthless character, having such a moral and intellectual development as Melancthon or Sully. In the heads of criminals, there is generally a great predominance of the organs of the propensities over those of the moral sentiments—a large mass of brain in the posterior and basilar regions, and a comparatively small portion in the frontal and coronal regions. Some malefactors, however, are drawn into crime more by unfavourable circumstances than by natural depravity; while other men, strongly disposed to crime, but rather fortunately situated in worldly matters, refrain, through dread of the consequences, from committing it. People with a good moral development, occasionally commit crimes from a diseased action of the brain. Such persons are virtually deranged, although this circumstance is not always taken into consideration.

What character results from a pretty equal development of the propensities, sentiments, and intellect?

It will be good, bad, or indifferent, according to the situation in which the individual is placed. If in favourable circumstances, well educated, and under the influence of good example, he may turn out a very fair member of society;

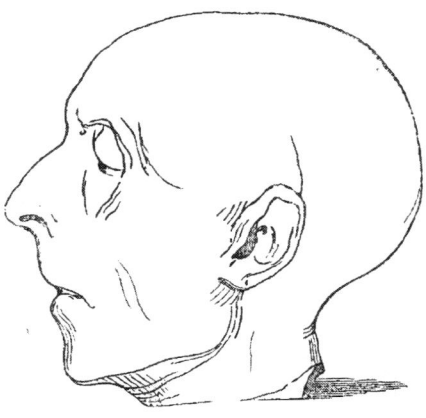

Sheridan.

if exposed to the contaminating influence of vice, he will be apt to run into it, and become a rogue. Sheridan was a man of this stamp. So long as he had plenty of money he maintained a fair character for respectability; but when his circumstances decayed, he sunk into disreputable and vicious courses, and died in poverty and contempt. Many with such a configuration of head have perished on the scaffold, owing to their being unfavourably situated for the manifestation of their moral sentiments, and but too favourably for the indulgence of the propensities. This remark applies to Maxwell who was executed at Dumfries for theft. In him, also, a pretty uniform balance of the three sets of faculties existed.

From what do such differences proceed?

From the particular faculties which are most exercised taking the lead. In virtuous society, the higher feelings, such as Benevolence, Veneration, and Conscientiousness, are cherished, and the lower ones, as Destructiveness, Combativeness, and Amativeness, repressed; whence the former (in a case where both are equally strong by nature) predominate. Reverse the case, and the predominance is given to the latter. No good example could ever have made a virtuous character of such a man as Bellingham, armed, as he was, with an enormous supremacy of the lower faculties; nor could any conceivable familiarity with scenes of vice have made a villain of Fenelon or Howard. Such a doctrine, some people may say, makes man a mere machine. With this the disciples of Gall have nothing to do. They simply reveal nature as they find it. Facts demonstrate that a certain physical organization is invariably accompanied with a particular mental constitution. It is the will of the Divine Being that such a correspondence should exist, and phrenologists are but the humble interpreters of His laws as they affect the brain. Let those whose cerebral system is happily constituted, thank the Almighty Power, from whom they have their being, that He has so beneficently endowed them; but let them deal gently with those whom it has been His pleasure to form after a less perfect model.

Is not one faculty modified by the influence of another?

This is true as respects the result of the faculty, but not as respects the force of the faculty itself. For instance, a man offends me, and my excited Destructiveness prompts me to knock him down; but I am restrained by Cautiousness from so doing. The desire to strike is here nowise lessened; in other words, the activity of Destructiveness is not abated: the result merely to which it would otherwise lead is modified.

Is the activity of one organ ever increased by that of another?

Undoubtedly. If we look at a beautiful child, we experience at once kindly feelings towards him, from Philoprogenitiveness and Ideality calling our Benevolence into active operation. If Ideality is offended by a loathsome reptile, Destructiveness is excited, and we are disposed to trample it under foot, however innoxious the creature may be. Conscientiousness, offended by false suspicions against one's self, excites Destructiveness. Dr. Combe suggests, that it is from the contiguity of the organs of Adhesiveness, Combativeness, and Destructiveness, that domestic dissensions are the most bitter and irreconcileable of any.[115] The latter organ is violently excited by drinking, which has led

---

[115] " A curious example of the effect of Benevolence in rousing Destructiveness, is furnished by the history of Montbar, a Frenchman, who was so furiously exasperated by reading, in early life, accounts of the cruelties of the Spaniards in America, that he joined the Bucaneers, a body of pirates long the scourge of navigators in the West Indies. So much, and so frequently did this man gall the Spaniards, during the whole of his life, that he acquired from them the name of ' the Exterminator.' Of course, the independent energy of his Destructiveness itself must have been very great."—*See an admirable paper by Mr. Robert Cox, in the Phrenological Journal*, vol. ix. p. 402.

some to conjecture, that this is owing to its being in the immediate neighbourhood of Alimentiveness, the organ which is peculiarly excited by intoxication. This doctrine, however, of one organ being stimulated from the contiguity of another, in an excited state, though highly plausible, is open to serious objections. If Alimentiveness, for instance, excite Destructiveness, why does not Destructiveness excite Alimentiveness, and thus render a man desirous to eat when in a passion?

What should be the main purposes of education?

To cultivate and direct the moral and intellectual faculties, by means of exercise, instruction, and example, and to repress, as much as possible, the undue activity of the lower feelings. In most people, the three classes of faculties are nearly on a par; and upon education and example does it greatly depend which shall take the lead in life.

How is Phrenology useful in education, seeing that a person's talents and dispositions may be ascertained without its aid?

The greater our knowledge of the mental faculties, the more perfectly are we made acquainted with the manner in which they ought to be cultivated and applied. Phrenology gives us this knowledge in a way superior to any other source of information, and, therefore, must be eminently useful in the education of youth. Independently of this, talents and dispositions are very far from being so easily found out as is sometimes imagined; and whatever tends to facilitate their discovery, must be looked upon as a matter of high importance. Both these purposes being served by Phrenology, its uses in education are sufficiently obvious.

Has the size of the lungs any influence on the brain's activity?

Doubtless it has. When the lungs are large, the blood is more highly vivified, the circulation stronger, and the brain nourished more completely, than when these organs are small. Byron was a middle-sized man, but his lungs were gigantic in their proportions; which may, perhaps, account in some degree for his astonishing cerebral activity. At the same time, it is not to be inferred, that because a man's respiratory organs are large, his brain will necessarily be an active one. All I mean to say is, that—other things being equal—a large-lunged man will display greater vigour and activity of mind than one in whom the lungs are small.

Have all kinds of food the same influence on the energy of the brain?

No. Animal food stimulates the cerebral structure, and contributes to its activity, much more than vegetable. If a person is fed too much on vegetable diet, the mental powers become enfeebled. In work-houses, where the inmates have poor diet, and that often not in sufficient quantity, there may be remarked a general want of vigour in the mind. Ill-fed children are far less likely to possess powerful intellects than those who are properly nourished. Man partaking of the qualities of a carnivorous and graminivorous animal, it was not the intention of nature that he should be restricted to a merely vegetable diet. From such a diet the brain does not receive sufficient stimulus, and is apt to fall into a torpid state. A considerable allowance of animal food is necessary, especially in temperate and cold climates, to excite the cerebral structure properly, and keep it in healthy and vigorous action. Still there is a limit which must not be transgressed. An undue quantity of such food over-stimulates the brain, particularly in the region of the propensities, and gives rise to improper action of these organs. The effect of animal diet taken in large quantities, is well exhibited in the ferocity with which dogs who are fed much upon it, are soon inspired.

Do phrenologists assign any organ for memory?

They do not. Memory is an attribute of all the intellectual faculties, and not a primitive mental power. If it were, a person whose memory was good for one thing, should possess it in equal perfection for all; but this is not the case. We meet with people who have a great memory for words, and an indifferent one for events; who recollect localities and forms accurately, but have little power of remembering music. This proves, that memory is not a separate faculty, and cannot have a special organ. A person with a good development of Language, has a memory for words; a second, with large Number, for numbers; a third, with large Tune, for music; and so on. Thus, memory is connected with all the intellectual faculties, and is merely one of the modes of their action.

What opinion would you form of a person who has a bad memory?

Either that his intellect, wholly or in part, has never been cultivated, or that it is naturally very common-place. Memory being the manifestation of vigorous faculties, it follows, that when it is bad, these faculties also must be deficient in energy, either from natural feebleness or want of exercise. No maxim is more false, than that " great wits have short memories." The memory of every man of talent is, by nature, a good one, in matters having relation to his talent. If he allows his faculties to rust, by not employing them, he has only himself to blame for his defective memory.

Why does memory so strikingly fail in old age?

Because the faculties, of which it is a mode of action, fail.

Are not Perception, Attention, and Conception, primitive mental powers?

The metaphysicians say so, but Phrenology denies the assertion. According to our doctrine, they are merely different modes of action of the knowing and reflecting faculties.

Perception is the lowest degree. If I hear a violin played in the street, my organ of Tune is stimulated, and I perceive the music. Attention is perception with an effort. If my Tune is in such a state of vigorous excitement as to enable me to compose or conceive music, the process of Conception then takes place, and the organ is in the highest state of activity. Perception, Attention, and Conception, therefore, are, like Memory, connected with all the intellectual faculties. They are simply particular states of activity of those faculties.

What is the cause of enthusiasm?

It may arise from various sources. Thus, when Tune is very large and active, the individual is enthusiastic about music; when Veneration and Wonder predominate, he is an enthusiast in religion; with Combativeness and Destructiveness greatly developed, he may be an enthusiastic soldier or prize-fighter. Ideality gives poetical enthusiasm, and also vivifies that arising from the other faculties. Large Hope, with small Cautiousness and Causality, produce the scheming enthusiast. And so on. In all, an active temperament is generally found.

Give a phrenological explanation of grief.

The faculties are so constituted with relation to external objects and occurrences, as to be affected agreeably by some of them, and the reverse by others. Acquisitiveness, for example, is gratified by pecuniary gain, and annoyed by loss: Adhesiveness delights in the society of a friend, and suffers pain at his death. Grief, then, is simply the painful affection of these or other faculties; and, while the excitement continues, no reasoning or consolation is able to root out the painful sensation from the mind. Grief is to Adhesiveness, or whatever organ is painfully affected, exactly what toothach is to the nerves of the teeth: when the excitement of these nerves subsides, so does the pain; and in like manner, when the irritated organs in the brain return to their habitual condition, the sorrow gives way to calmness and peace.

What is envy?

It is the result of Destructiveness and offended Self-Esteem acting in combination, and producing hatred in consequence of another's success.

What is selfishness?

The quality of mind resulting from great Acquisitiveness and Self-Esteem, with deficient Benevolence.

What does common sense depend upon?

Upon a harmonious arrangement of the Propensities, Sentiments, and Intellect—where all are so equally balanced as not to interfere with or run counter to one another. General Washington was an admirable instance of this beautiful adaptation. Strictly speaking, he had no very shining qualities, and little of what might be called genius. As a general, he was nothing to Hannibal, Napoleon, or Frederic of Prussia; as a philosopher, he could not be named with Franklin, and as a legislator he has been often surpassed. Whence, then, arose his greatness? The secret lay in his admirable common sense: his judgment, from the manner in which his faculties were combined, was surprisingly sound; his moral sentiments were elevated and noble; and his propensities were finely kept in subordination. This combination rendered him a truly great man, and as such he has been universally recognized by the world. Common sense is a rare quality, and many persons are said to possess it who have no claim whatever to such a distinction.

What does indolence arise from?

From inactivity of brain, either natural to the person, and in constant or frequent existence; or accidental, the result of indigestion, bad health, or some other temporary cause.

What is the origin of insipidity of character?

It is connected with an inert brain and small Destructiveness, and is most apt to accompany the lymphatic temperament.

How do you explain the phenomena of laughter and weeping?

It is not easy to determine why certain mental states give rise to these and other bodily affections. The following are my views, and, after all, they do not throw much light on the subject:—When certain parts of the body are affected in certain modes, other parts are simultaneously affected, in virtue of a mysterious law of the animal constitution, called the law of sympathy. When an irritating substance is thrown into the eyes, or drawn up into the nostrils, the diaphragm and pectoral muscles act violently, and produce sneezing. When the lungs are irritated by mucus or other foreign agents introduced into them, a similar result follows, and we cough. When the organ of Destructiveness is roused, the facial muscles are affected in such a manner as to give the countenance the natural language of rage. A man who suffers acute pain, suddenly inflicted, screams or howls. Terror makes the knees smite each other. In the same way, it appears, that laughter is the natural language of highly pleasurable affections of the cerebral organs. Tickle a child, and he laughs immoderately. Give him a piece of money; praise him; play a trick before him; please him in any way, and the result is laughter. Even Destructiveness has its sardonic laugh. On the other hand, weeping generally proceeds from disagreeable affections of the organs. Beat, scold, or thwart a child, and he cries bitterly. The loss of friends is a standard source of weeping. Adults are less easily moved to tears than children; the cause of which seems to be, that they are more able to regulate the action of their faculties. There is another source of tears, in moods called *pathetic*, which are rather agreeable than the reverse. We weep on reading an affecting story, such as "Julia de Roubigné," and at beholding a pathetic play such as "Romeo and Juliet," and the feeling is, upon the whole, a pleasurable and not a painful one.

What is the phrenological theory of jealousy?

This state of mind is a combination of selfishness with suspicion; that is to say, it proceeds from Self-Esteem, Secretiveness, and Cautiousness, in combination with Acquisitiveness, or some other faculty desiring enjoyment.

What does hypocrisy result from?

From Secretiveness in excess, with deficient Conscientiousness. To persist in a course of hypocrisy, a great deal of Firmness is requisite.

From what does credulity proceed?

It arises, generally, from too much Veneration, Wonder, or Hope, but its direction varies according as one or other of these organs is large. Veneration renders people credulous with respect to what is affirmed by those whom they revere, Hope with respect to the occurrence of wished-for events, and Wonder with respect to whatever is marvellous or mysterious. Very large Self-Esteem, it may be farther observed, disposes a flattered person to credulity, by giving him the idea that he really merits the adulation bestowed. Credulity is, in a great measure, counteracted by a powerful and well-instructed understanding.

What is the cause of incredulity?

A deficiency of the organs which dispose to credulity, is one cause. It may, however, arise, in many cases, from ignorance. Thus, an illiterate clown laughs in your face, if you tell him that the earth is shaped like an orange, and moves round the sun; or that the stars which we see twinkling in the firmament, are, each of them, a great deal larger than the earth.

I

Some people are exceedingly nice, dainty, and finical, in all they say or do: What is the cause of this?

It probably arises from a great devolpment of Individuality and Order, particularly where the organs of the Reflective Faculties are moderate, and the person is not familiar with science and the more arduous pursuits of human life.

From what do impudence and forwardness proceed?

An individual in whom Combativeness and Self-Esteem are large, and Secretiveness, Cautiousness, Love of Approbation, Benevolence, and Conscientiousness moderate, will certainly be forward and impudent. Knowledge of the world, by teaching the insignificance of self, tends to allay impudence.

What is the cause of frivolity?

Frivolity results from a small and very active brain. A large-brained person may be dull, but he can hardly be frivolous.

What is the cause of presence of mind?

Its chief elements are Combativeness, Firmness, Secretiveness, Self-Esteem, Hope, and probably Individuality. The first two give courage and resolution to meet the unexpected contingency; the third enables the person to conceal his feelings of alarm or astonishment, if he has any; the fourth and fifth inspire him with confidence, and the last communicates quickness of observation, which will make him notice every thing at a glance, and thus give him an opportunity of promptly encountering whatever may occur.

Why are religious people of excellent moral character sometimes seized with the distressful idea of their extreme unworthiness in the sight of God?

This arises from great Veneration, and small Hope and Self-Esteem. If to such a combination there is added a large development of Conscientiousness, the person will be apt to accuse himself of heinous offences against the Deity, and be haunted with the idea of eternal punishment. Fanaticism and every form of religious enthusiasm and insanity are to be traced, without difficulty, to the immoderate or ill-regulated action of some of the organs of the brain.

Some people acquire knowledge readily, and as readily forget it; in others the reverse happens: How do you explain such differences?

It is supposed that they are occasioned by difference of quality of the brain, an active temperament giving quickness of memory, and an inactive one rendering it, *cæteris paribus*, slow but retentive. The causes, however, of these and some other differences of memory are still under investigation.

Why are women's prejudices stronger than men's?

Partly because in the female brain the reflective organs are smaller, and partly because women mingle less with the world, and therefore enjoy fewer opportunities of having their prepossessions effaced by the friction of society. If men would address themselves more to the intellect, and less to the vanity of females, the latter would not only get rid of many prejudices, but occupy a far higher place as intellectual beings than they can possibly do in the present constitution of things.[116] Queen Elizabeth, and the Catherines of Russia, are striking examples of female vigour of

---

[116] The present century is more distinguished than any which has preceded it for the production of eminent females. Witness Baillie, Hemans, Bowles, and Landon, in poetry—Edgeworth, Ferriar, and the Porters, in prose, fiction—De Stael and Martineau in political disquisition—and the illustrious name of Sommerville, in the physical sciences. Such instances as the latter three, sufficiently demonstrate that even in those walks where the male intellect is supposed to be peculiarly strong, it may occasionally be rivalled by that of the other sex; and that it would be so much oftener, were women more favourably circumstanced for the development of their energies, can hardly admit of a doubt. Still, in a general sense, the superior size of the male brain will always give that sex a superiority.

intellect; and the present age boasts of many illustrious examples, though in a different sphere of life, and in a different walk.

May activity of brain exist with little power?

It often does. A small brain in combination with a high nervous or sanguine temperament, will display activity; but, from its deficient dimensions, power, or intensity of function, will be awanting. To display the latter quality, a large brain is necessary. Dr. Spurzheim was of opinion, that length of fibre in the brain produces activity, and that breadth communicates power.

May a person of common-place talent show power of mind?

He may, but it will be the power of the propensities, and not of the intellect. A dog-fighter or an ignorant hackney-coachman, may, in this sense, be said to show more cerebral vigour than a Shakspeare or a Bacon.

Have all nations the same tendency to emancipate themselves from superstition?

They have not. Other things, such as education and intercourse with other nations, being equal, those nations in which the reflective organs exist in greatest perfection, will most readily unthrall themselves from superstitious absurdities. The difficulty of getting quit of them, however, must be doubly great, even with good intellect, where a large development of Wonder and Veneration is common, as is the case with the Hindoos and other Orientals.

What nations possess the most intellectual form of head?

Those undoubtedly which are of that variety denominated the white or Caucasian. Nations with this form of head, have a strong tendency to progress in refinement; while most other races remain in their primitive state of barbarism, or, at most, never go much beyond it. If the Negroes, the American Indians, the Hottentots, and other savage tribes, had possessed the European form of brain, they would have civilized themselves many centuries ago, and been in every respect on a par with the whites. On the contrary, they have done nothing for themselves, and the little that has been done for them is the work of others. Some of these races are so deficient in intellect, that it has been found impracticable to educate them: such seems to be the case with the aborigines of New Holland, Van Dieman's Land, and the United States of America. In the white races, on the contrary, even though placed under the most unfavourable circumstances for moral and intellectual improvement, as in Turkey and modern Greece, we can see the seeds of all the noblest faculties of our nature; and no sooner is the dead weight of tyranny and superstition which prevents their growth removed, than they burst into all the promise of a fruitful harvest. The Mongolian form of head has an intellectual development between that of the Caucasian and Ethiopian; and, accordingly, we find that some of the nations which possess it, such as the Chinese and Japanese, have made considerable strides in civilization; but having attained this, they continue stationary, as we at present find them, and seem incapable of advancing a step farther, at least by their own efforts. When the frontal and coronal regions of the brain are generally well developed in a nation, its tendency will be towards intellectual and moral pursuits; and unless some strong external counteracting agency is at work, the people will speedily become civilized. Where the posterior and basilar regions predominate, the nation will be governed by the lower propensities, and civilization be an imperfect process. In the following sketches we have a Carib and a Teutonic head: the latter is the type of head prevailing among the civilized nations of Europe, and its immense superiority in the regions of sentiment and intellect is obvious at a single glance. Ungovernable propensities, and wretched morality and intelligence, are the distinguishing features of a people with the Carib form of head.

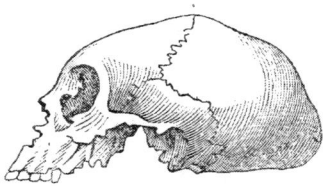
Carib.

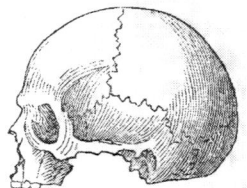
Teutonic.

Are any of the lower animals gifted with reason?

Some of them are so, although it is common to deny them the possession of this quality. If a dog leaps upon a table and is well whipped for doing so, why does he cease to repeat the offence? Simply because his reason tells him that a repetition of it will lead to renewed punishment.

Have all portions of the human brain corresponding portions in the brains of the lower animals?

No. The convolutions in which Veneration, Wonder, Conscientiousness, and Ideality reside, are peculiar to the human brain.

Is not Phrenology a difficult science, seeing that it requires attention to so many circumstances, such as age, temperament, health of brain, and education?

Phrenology is not difficult to those who will take the trouble of studying it as it ought to be studied; and even if it were difficult, this is no argument against its utility and truth. With regard to the number of circumstances to which it demands attention, the science is not otherwise situated than any other. They are part and parcel of itself; they are certain of the conditions that belong to it: and to study phrenology without attending to them, would be as absurd as to attempt to get a proper knowledge of physiology without anatomy, or of astronomy without mathematics. Phrenology regards not merely the form and size of the brain, as is often ignorantly supposed, but also the diversified causes which affect its activity and vigour, the laws according to which those causes operate, and, in general every circumstance tending to influence the mental powers.[117]

Does not Phrenology lead to materialism?

If by materialism is meant the identity of mind and matter, it leads to nothing of the kind; phrenologists expressly declaring their belief that the brain is not the mind, but simply the organized medium through which, in this life, it manifests itself. Gall and Spurzheim were immaterialists, and so are the most eminent of their disciples, including Mr. Combe.[118]

---

[117] The opponents of Phrenology are continually disregarding these conditions. Phrenologists positively declare, that no correct inference can be deduced in cases of old age and diseased brain; yet we had lately the skull of Dean Swift brought forward as an evidence against the science, in the face of the notorious fact, that the Dean died at the age of seventy-eight, and had been subject to loss of memory, and frantic fits of passion, eleven years before his death, and that the last five years of his life were passed in idiocy. The most amusing thing connected with such cases is, that phrenologists are accused of always having a loop-hole to escape by. If they had made it one of the principles of the science, that from an old and diseased brain, it could be inferred what sort of character the individual possessed in youth and health, and if such a test were found, on trial, completely to fail, the only inference would be, that the phrenologists were wrong; but when they distinctly state the conditions of their science, what right has any man, in testing it, to overlook these conditions, and then set up a cry about loop-holes? If a medical man were asked how much laudanum might be safely given to an adult, and were to answer, forty drops, would he be responsible if the person who asked him were to give the same quantity to a child, and thus destroy it? As well might this person accuse him of getting out by a loop-hole, when he declared that the dose was distinctly mentioned as for an adult, and not for a child. If the opponents of Phrenology choose to try this science by rules which its professors positively renounce, they are acting a part equally illogical and absurd.

[118] The following sensible remarks from a religious publication, show the absurdity of this charge. "This doctrine may, or it may not, be true,

Does Phrenology, by making dispositions depend upon the shape of the brain, lead to the destruction of responsibility?

Phrenology leaves the question of responsibility precisely as it found it.[119] No person now pretends that every one is, by nature, equally talented and virtuous. The Scriptures distinctly recognize a difference of moral and intellectual gifts, when they announce, that "unto whomsoever much is given, of him shall be much required;" clearly declaring, that God did not make every one alike, and that He would exact from us in proportion to the degree with which we were gifted with His bounties—demanding one talent from one man, and two from another. The Scriptures thus point

---

but it certainly does not appear to us to be fairly liable to the charge of materialism. That certain cerebral organs are connected with certain mental faculties does not appear to us to involve materialism, any more than the fact that the eye is the organ of seeing, or the ear of hearing; certainly not more than the old and very widely entertained supposition that the brain is the seat of thought. That the soul is connected with a set of material organs, through which it holds communion with the external world, and that that connexion, though it may undergo very great modifications, is destined to endure for ever, are doctrines which nobody either denies, or supposes to involve materialism. And what more materialism is involved in the supposition that a particular organ is connected with a particular faculty, we do not see.—*Edinburgh Christian Instructor.*

119 I have elsewhere spoken of the attacks made by some persons upon modern geologists, on the ground of their discoveries being hostile to religion. The Rev. Mr. Sedgwick chastises the presumptuous ignorance of these individuals with well-merited severity. "There is another class of men," says he, "who pursue geology by a nearer road, and are guided by a different light. Well-intentioned they may be, but they have betrayed no small self-sufficiency, along with a shameful want of knowledge of the fundamental facts they presume to write about; hence they have dishonoured the literature of this country by *Mosaic Geology, Scripture Geology,* and other works of cosmogony with kindred titles, wherein they have overlooked the end and aim of revelation, tortured the book of life out of its proper meaning, and wantonly contrived to bring about a collision between natural phenomena and the Word of God." These remarks apply with equal force to the attempt which has more than once been made to place Phrenology at variance with religion.

out a marked difference of endowment among men, and Phrenology does no more. For such differences there must be some cause, and the science in question ascribes them to peculiarities of physical organization in the brain; but to say that this leads to irresponsibility more than any other doctrine which admits of natural differences of mental endowment, is to assert a palpable and childish absurdity.[120]

Matter being subject to death, Phrenology, by connecting the mind with it, surely militates against the doctrine of the immortality of the soul?

In reality, it does nothing of the kind. All that Phrenologists contend for is, that in the present life, material organs are necessary for the mental manifestations, just as eyes and ears are necessary for sight and hearing, or a stomach for digestion. The opposite doctrine, that in this state of being the mind acts independently of organization, does, in reality, militate against the immortality of the soul, and degrades the mind to a level with the dust; for it makes the soul a changeable essence, subject to infinite alterations—

---

[120] " Simple and unprejudiced observation of human life is, we imagine, sufficient to prove the innateness of the faculties, and that the individuals of the race are endowed with them in different degrees: Phrenology merely confirms the results of observation, and elucidates the causes of perceived and indubitable phenomena. It is absurd, therefore, to object to Phrenology in particular on the score of necessity, and to allow the other systems to remain undisturbed as perfectly harmless. If the new system leads to necessity, it is impossible to avoid the conclusion, that the old systems lead to it also. Christianity itself—which teaches the innateness of human dispositions, and the inherent variety of their force among individuals—which teaches that ' the tree is known by his fruit,' and that ' a good man, out of the good treasure of the heart, bringeth forth good things, and an evil man, out of the evil treasure, bringeth forth evil things ' (Matt. xii. 33, 35.), —Christianity itself, we say, is equally liable to the charge. The objectors ought to be aware, that if they could prove Phrenology to have, in this respect, an evil tendency, they would, at the very same time, inevitably demonstrate the evil tendency of the Christian religion. Unless they are prepared for this result, which possibly has not occurred to them, they will act wisely in quitting the field."—*Phrenological Journal*, vol. viii. p. 547.

weak and fickle in infancy, vigorous in manhood, imbecile in old age, and not unfrequently afflicted with idiocy and madness. If an immaterial spirit be liable to such changes, why may it not be subject to death itself? Those, therefore, who oppose Phrenology on the above ground, are casting aside a doctrine which does not bear against the immortality of the soul, and blindly grasping at one which almost necessarily infers its destructibility.

Is not madness a disease of the mind?

Not such, properly speaking, although it is customary so to consider it. Madness arises from a distempered state of the organic apparatus by which the mind works; it is a symptom of diseased brain, just as indigestion is of disordered stomach. Considered as a separate entity, we may as well speak of the death of the mind, as of its disease. In short, we ascribe madness to an unhealthy state of the instrument which the mind makes use of; as, in looking through a telescope, the glass of which is soiled, we see objects obscurely, not from any defect of the objects themselves, but from their being seen through an imperfect medium.

Can the particular form of madness under which a person labours, be surmised by examination of his head?

This may often be done with wonderful accuracy. If an organ in the head of an insane person predominates very much over the others, we may infer, with every chance of being right in our conjecture, that this organ is in a state of morbid excitement, and that therein lies the disease. If a patient in a mad-house is presented to us with an inordinate development of the organ of Cautiousness, there is every likelihood that he labours under excessive apprehension, and great lowness of spirits. If with this we find Veneration amply displayed, he probably is afflicted with religious melancholy. If Self-Esteem is large, he, in all likelihood, supposes himself some great personage; and so on with respect to other organs—the largest being always the most likely to get into a state of disease.

What class of persons are likely to be the most bitter enemies of Phrenology?

Those who themselves possess a defective moral or intellectual development. Some men of great talent and perfect integrity, have opposed the science through ignorance; but their opposition, so far from being of an immitigable character, would disappear at once before the light of a proper knowledge of the subject. This has already happened in many instances; and some who formerly ridiculed Phrenology as an idle chimera, are now among the most able and enthusiastic of its supporters. Where the development, however, is morally or intellectually defective, the opposition will continue, in the face of any evidence, however strong.[121]

What is the main object of Phrenology?

This is made sufficiently apparent by the whole tenor of the preceding pages, and hardly admits of a condensed reply. It may be stated briefly, that the purpose of the science is to give man a knowledge of himself; to point out

---

[121] " Neither Homer's Thersites, whose cranium was 'misshapen,' nor any of Shakspeare's personages, with 'foreheads villanously low,' could have been easily proselyted to the doctrines of Phrenology. The reason is obvious. Their own heads would not have 'passed muster.' Their belief, therefore, would have been *self-condemnatory*. And as no man is bound, in common law, to give evidence against himself, neither is it very consistent with the laws of human nature, for any one to believe, more especially to avow his belief, to his own disparagement. As the hump-backed, knock-kneed, and bandy-legged, have an instinctive hostility to the exercise of gymnastics, it is scarcely to be expected that the flat-heads, apple-heads, and sugar-loaf-heads, will be favourably disposed to that of Phrenology. Nor will those whose brains are so ponderous behind, and light before, that their heads seem in danger of tilting backward."—*Professor Caldwell's New Views of Penitentiary Discipline, &c.* Philadelphia, 1829.

the true method of studying the mind, and of directing and applying its energies to proper uses. Phrenology is a study which tends eminently to virtue; in particular, it teaches toleration and mutual forbearance. By demonstrating the natural variety of human dispositions and talents, and the innateness of our strongest motives, it loudly urges us to judge charitably of the actions of others, and to make allowance for their imperfections—to lay upon no individual more than he is able to bear, and to desist from the mad attempts which have so often been made to assimilate to one common standard the opinions of the whole community. On the philosophy of education, and on the treatment of criminals and the insane, Phrenology throws a flood of light.

APPENDIX.

No. I.

THE relative size of the different organs is designated by the Edinburgh phrenologists as follows:—

1.	8, rather small.	15.
2, idiocy.	9.	16, rather large.
3.	10, moderate.	17.
4, very small.	11.	18, large.
5.	12, rather full.	19.
6, small.	13.	20, very large.
7.	14, full.	

The figure 12, therefore, annexed to the name of an organ, signifies that it is "rather full;" 19 means that it is between "large" and "very large;" and so on.

The temperament of the individual whose head is examined, is also noted; and his education, as well as the circumstances in which he has been surrounded, ought to be inquired into.

No. II.

PHRENOLOGICAL ANALYSIS OF THE CHARACTER OF GEORGE CAMPBELL, EXECUTED FOR MURDER.

ON the 29th of September, 1835, George Campbell was executed at Glasgow for murder. As the crime was characterised by peculiarly atrocious features, and his conduct, on receiving sentence, marked by unparalleled ferocity, I was anxious to ascertain how far the developments, in a phrenological point of view, harmonised with so strongly marked and singular a character. Having asked permission of the Magistrates to take a cast of his head after death, the request was, in the most liberal manner, at once granted, and a cast was accordingly taken. On examining this cast, I, as well as every one conversant with Phrenology by whom it was seen, perceived at once that it, in a most remarkable degree, confirmed the doctrines of Gall. Conceiving, however, that a previous knowledge of the individual might have had some influence in swaying our judgments, and making us see a greater analogy between the physical organization and the mental character than was actually warranted by circumstances, I came to the resolution of sending the cast to an eminent phrenologist in Edinburgh, for the purpose of learning what inference he—without any bias, and in perfect ignorance of the person from whom it was taken—would draw from it. To prevent the possibility of any suspicion being aroused on his part, the cast was forwarded, *not to him*, but to another gentleman, who was requested to deliver it into his hands, without saying whose head it was, by whom it was sent, or from what quarter it came. To make assurance doubly sure, that portion of the neck at the angle of the jaw, marked by the pressure of the rope, was carefully removed. No external mark was thus left to indicate that the person had perished by strangulation, nor did the countenance display the slightest appearance of violent death. This fact may be verified by any person who chooses to examine the cast. The gentleman to whom it was sent, performed his part with scrupulous fidelity, and handed the cast to the object of its destination. " Mr. ———," says he, " had no information except what he has prefixed to his paper, and the knowledge of the fact that the cast was that of a dead man." This information refers to the age, temperament, and education of the criminal—circumstances which must, in the generality of cases, be known before any thing like a just deduction can be drawn.

Campbell was of Irish parentage. In appearance he was a good-looking and rather prepossessing young man. In stature he stood about five feet seven inches, was cleanly made, and rather athletic. While very young he entered the army, where he remained seven years. Of his *general* conduct there, I am unable to learn any thing that can be depended upon; suffice it to say, that he was at one time severely flogged for striking his sergeant. On leaving the army, he went to his father's house, but soon left it in consequence of some family quarrels. He then took up his lodgings with a woman named Hanlin, with whose daughter (and with the mother also, if accounts can be trusted,) he lived in a state of fornication. Hanlin's house was a most abandoned one. Lord Meadowbank, one of the judges before whom Campbell was tried, pronounced it, with great truth and force of language, "a den of infamy, and the old woman the presiding demon of the place." It was for murdering this woman that Campbell paid the forfeit of his life. He had frequently threatened to murder her, and one day carried his purpose into effect, by literally, and in the most determined and ferocious manner, trampling her to death. After committing this crime, he made no attempt to escape, but went and informed the neighbours that the woman had killed herself by drinking. He was apprehended, tried, *and convicted, very much to his own astonishment;* and when sentence was passed upon him, he burst forth into a volley of imprecations against the judges, such as never before polluted a court of justice—threatening, at the same time, with horrible language, to strike the criminal officers who offered to remove him. Those present on the occasion describe his conduct as unutterably horrible and disgusting. On being taken to the condemned cell, he seemed more attentive to his food than any thing else, complained bitterly of the jail allowance, and expressed great satisfaction when supplied with food of a better quality. He was grossly ignorant, obdurate, and impenitent. The respectable Catholic clergymen by whom he was attended (for he belonged to the Church of Rome) had great difficulty in making him comprehend almost any thing. To the last he denied his guilt. He may have acknowledged it privately to his confessor, but this, of course, is not known. He was vain of his person, and inclined to dress neatly. As a proof of this, he devoted a quarter of an hour, immediately previous to his execution, to curling his hair. On mounting the scaffold, he displayed wonderful firmness, walking erectly, tossing his head back in a theatrical manner, and having a bold swaggering appearance. All accounts agree in representing his life, so far as it is known, as rude, turbulent, and debauched. To the young woman with whom he cohabited, he was attached, although this did not prevent him from occasionally beating her, I suppose in his drunken fits. The attachment was mutual on her part, and remained unweakened even after he murdered her mother; she visited him in jail subsequently to his condemnation, and seemed much affected by his situation. Having made these preliminary remarks, let us now turn to the phrenological analysis. It is as follows, and sufficiently vindicates the skill and acumen of the gentleman by whom it was made :—

Plaster cast—size a little above average—temperament nervous-bilious—age 25—uneducated—dissipated.

DEVELOPMENT.

Instinct of food, (Alimentiveness) large,	18
Amativeness, large,	19
Philoprogenitiveness, very large,	20
Concentrativeness, full,	14

APPENDIX.

Adhesiveness, large, ... 19
Combativeness, very large, ... 20
Destructiveness, very large, ... 20
Secretiveness, very large, ... 20
Acquisitiveness, large, ... 18
Constructiveness, small, ... 8
Self-Esteem, extra large, ... 22
Love of Approbation, very large, . . . 20
Cautiousness, rather large, ... 16
Benevolence, moderate, ... 11
Veneration, large, ... 18
Firmness, very large, ... 20
Hope, large, ... 18
Conscientiousness, rather full, ... 13
Wonder, large, ... 18
Ideality, moderate, ... 11
Wit, moderate, ... 11
Imitation, rather full, ... 12

INTELLECT.

Individuality, rather large, ... 17
Form, full, ... 14
Size, full, ... 15
Weight, full, ... 14
Colouring, full, ... 14
Locality, large, ... 19
Number, rather full, ... 12
Order, large, ... 18
Eventuality, full, ... 15
Time, large, ... 19
Tune, large, ... 18
Language, rather large, ... 16
Comparison, moderate, ... 10
Causality, moderate, ... 11

The following is an accurate profile of the head from which these developments were taken:—

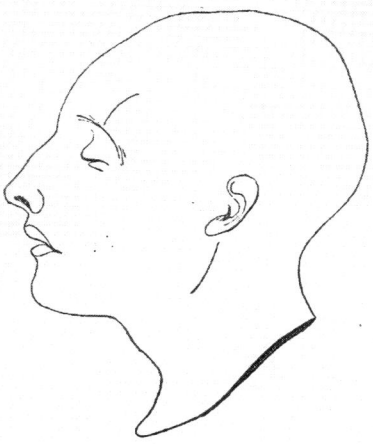

CHARACTER INFERRED.

I was struck with the resemblance of this cast to that of the too famous Thurtell, in the Phrenological Society's collection; only that Thurtell's Benevolence was larger, and his head generally larger; and on turning to the development preserved of Thurtell in the Phrenological Journal, vol. I. page 328, (but not till I had noted down that of the cast sent me,) I found them to agree to a great extent. The individual from whom this cast was taken, being uneducated, and having possessed an active temperament, would give unrestrained vent to a degree of animalism and selfishness, which must have rendered him a nuisance to his neighbourhood. He has the organization of gross sensuality in all its three points. Even when sober, he had a tendency to brawling and bullying—a compound of impudent assurance, self-conceit, vanity, insolence, tyranny, obstinacy, violence, and cruelty; but, when drunk, a strait-waiscoat, or a cell in the police-office, would be absolutely necessary. He would be loud, boisterous, opinionative, and contentious, and his oaths and imprecations would be horrible; while his abuse would have in it an energy, malignity, and grossness, peculiarly his own. His selfishness would be unmitigated; grasping, without ever giving, would characterise him. His indifference to the misfortunes or sufferings of others would be marked; and scenes of suffering, such as executions, floggings, surgical operations, prize and cock fights, would greatly delight him. A single word, which he felt as slighting or ridiculing him, would be returned by a blow; but many an insult he would put on others, and in many a brawl he would be engaged. Nevertheless, he would not expose himself to unnecessary danger, but would calculate his adversary's strength before he proceeded to beat and bruise him or her; for his utter want of refinement and generosity would make no difference between sex or age, saving always the very young—for the only soft corner of his heart seems to have been love of children. He was cunning, and probably a measureless liar, both in his vain-glorious boastings, and for all other selfish ends. He was a plotter and manœuvrer; but although, from miserable reasoning powers, his schemes would be ill laid, he would have great pride in being thought a "deep dog." He was superstitious, a lover of the marvellous, and accessible to religious terrors; a *ghost* would settle him in his most boisterous moments. He would court society, and dislike solitude, seeking, of course, to be always the cock of the company; for there would be about him a great share of vulgar self-importance.

The knowing faculties seem good, and must have given considerable aptness and quickness. The Locality would give a roaming turn, and a knowledge of places. There must have been order and arrangement, which might show themselves in neatness and tidiness in dress. There is Music, or the love of it strong; and Time so largely endowed as not only to aid Music, but to give the power of telling the hour at any time without looking at the clock. The reflecting faculties are very poor indeed, which would produce a deficiency in sense, and an utter blindness to the simplest consequences. This defect would render abortive many a plan to deceive. Gambling and betting would have for this unfortunately organized being peculiar charms. He loved money, and would not be scrupulous about the means of getting it; while every farthing of it would go for selfish and chiefly sensual indulgences.

The cast appearing to have been taken after death, I asked and was informed that the individual is dead, and "has ceased from troubling;" and I congratulate all who knew him on the riddance. I should like to learn how he died—it could not be peacefully in his bed. Query—Was he hanged for beating out some one's brains, or otherwise murdering with ruthless brutality?

If such was his fate, I have only to say, that in that enlightened system of criminal treatment to which the country is coming, because *it must*, it needed not to have been so. A penitentiary department will come to be alloted for the constitutionally violent, brutal, and cruel, who will be put within walls for a long course of reformatory education on the first conviction by which their dangerous character is clearly proved. In a penitentiary, founded on the humane principle of reformation without inflictive vengeance, even such a being as this might have been humanized : at least, he would not have been permitted to annoy and endanger society, by a long course of violence—to end, perhaps, in murder.

REMARKS ON THE FOREGOING BY R. MACNISH.

I am doubtful whether Secretiveness and Acquisitiveness are so large as is given here. The thickness of the temporal muscle not being evident from a cast, has probably led the very able writer of the foregoing to over-rate them. He seems also to have made both Time and Tune larger than is justified by the appearance of the cast. Some, who have seen the cast, have objected that the distance from the ear to Individuality is larger than we might have been prepared for; but Phrenologists have long ceased to regard that measurement as any indication of the power of the intellect. The distance may be caused by a large middle lobe of the brain, as is the case in the present instance. The proper way to ascertain the point, is to look how far forward the anterior lobe projects from Constructiveness. The great size of Combativeness and Destructiveness (both 20) uncontrolled by his Benevolence, (which ranks only so high as 11,) and called into fierce action by liquor, easily accounts for the murder. His astonishment at the verdict of "guilty" probably arose from deficiency in the power of understanding the force of testimony, owing to the smallness of the reflecting organs. Ignorant people are very apt to indulge in absurd hopes. His great Love of Approbation, and his large Order, sufficiently explain the foppish freak of arranging his hair in curls at such a time, as well as the marked neatness of his dress as he appeared upon the scaffold. It is difficult to say what his religious feelings might have been, as probably his mind was never directed to religion till after he was condemned. His denial of the crime makes good his claim to the character of a liar. His Love of Approbation (20) would induce him to make it appear that he was innocent, and his Conscientiousness (only 13) would be no match for this strong feeling. The affection of the woman for him was very natural. He was a good-looking fellow, and was doubtless so much attached to her by his large Adhesiveness as to display affection when in good humour ; and when strong marks of affection are bestowed on a woman, she is certain, in most cases, to return it. The organ on which the Instinct of Food is conceived to depend, is as large as 18, which perhaps may explain his conduct with respect to the jail provisions, already alluded to, as well as his fondness for liquor. His good Time and Tune would probably give him a fondness for dancing, for which his figure was well adapted: but whether he really was given to this amusement, I have not been able to learn; that he was so, however, I have very little doubt. His great Amativeness (19) was sufficiently apparent, in the circumstances of his sensual career.

Altogether, the head of this man is such, that no good phrenologist, would hesitate one moment to say that the lower propensities must have been very predominant, prevailing lamentably over the Intellect and Moral Sentiments. His mode of life was extremely unfavourable to the exercise of the two latter, and must have tended to give to the first an enormous preponderance. Ignorance and dissipation acting together on such a mind, could hardly lead to any other result than the gallows. The analysis, to which I have ventured to add these observations, will speak for itself. It is perhaps one of the most skilful displays of phrenological acumen of which we have any record, and speaks volumes for the science. Wherever the man's character was known, the inference accords most minutely with it; and there is every reason to suppose, that, were those points cleared up, of which we are still ignorant, the correspondence between them and the deduction would be not less striking. The concluding paragraph of the analysis is most important, and well worthy the attention of legislators.

No. III.

ANOTHER CASE IN WHICH THE NATURAL DISPOSITIONS AND TALENTS WERE INFERRED FROM A CAST OF A HEAD.

About four years ago, a cast of a head was sent to Mr. Combe, by a gentleman residing at a considerable distance from Edinburgh, with a letter expressing "a strong curiosity to know what idea you will form of the party, without any previous hint of his character, and merely by examining his head. I may mention simply," continues the writer of the letter, "that the head is that of an uneducated person. If you will be so good as write me what you think, I shall return you an answer at length, stating as fully as I can, what I conceive to be the real character, intellectual and moral, of the individual. Of this man I can speak minutely. He is a very marked character; and, so far as I know Phrenology, his head is a complete index of himself." No other particulars were furnished.

Mr. Combe's engagements preventing him from undertaking this task, he put the cast into the hands of James Simpson, Esq., who examined it carefully, and drew out the following document:—

APPENDIX. 213

Cast of the head of an uneducated man, seemingly under middle life—general size of head very large—temperament not discoverable from the cast.

MEASUREMENT.

From spinal process of occipital bone to Individuality, 8¼
    Concentrativeness to Comparison, . . . 8
    Hole of ear to occipital spine, ... 4½
    Do. to Individuality, . . . 5¼
    Do. to Firmness, . . . 6⅔
    Destructiveness to Destructiveness, . . 6
    Secretiveness to Secretiveness, . . . 6⅕
    Cautiousness to Cautiousness, . . 6
    Ideality to Ideality, ... 4½
    Constructiveness to Constructiveness, . . 5⅓
    Philoprogenitiveness to Individuality, . . 8⅔
    Anterior lobe of the brain, rather large.
    Portion of brain above Cautiousness, moderate.
    Do. above Causality, moderate.

DEVELOPMENT.

Amativeness, large, ... 19
Philoprogenitiveness, very large, ... 20
Concentrativeness, large, ... 19
Adhesiveness, large, ... 18
Combativeness, large, ... 18
Destructiveness, large, ... 18
Secretiveness, large, ... 19
Acquisitiveness, large, ... 19
Constructiveness, full, ... 14
Self-Esteem, very large, ... 20
Love of Approbation, rather large, ... 16
Cautiousness, rather large, ... 16
Benevolence, moderate, ... 10
Veneration, full, ... 14
Firmness, large, ... 19
Conscientiousness, moderate, ... 10
Hope, full, ... 14
Wonder, full, ... 14
Ideality, rather full, ... 12
Wit, rather full, ... 12
Imitation, full, ... 15
Individuality, large, ... 18

APPENDIX.

Form, rather large,	16
Size, full,	14
Weight, moderate,	11
Colouring, small,	7
Locality, rather large,	17
Number, rather small,	8
Order, rather small,	6
Eventuality, rather large,	17
Time, rather large,	16
Tune, rather full,	13
Language, moderate,	10
Comparison, full,	14
Causality, full,	14

INFERENCES.

Mr. ―――― says he knows this individual well. I fear that, if he has had much to do with him, he knows him *too well*. His enormous head must give him great *power of character*, and I wish I could say that that power is all in the direction of good. Without education, and, of course, in inferior society, I could not answer for this individual not running headlong into the coarsest vicious indulgences. The *animal* endowment is excessive; and although the *intellectual* is very considerable, the *moral* is sadly deficient. The Amativeness is very great, and it is scarcely to be expected that it has been restrained from coarse and selfish indulgence. The individual may have married, and may have continued in the state as well as entered into it, and loved wife and children, (the latter passionately;) but he would usually be a harsh and tyrannical head of a family. He is loud, domineering, and assuming, and probably abusive and imprecatory. He is deficient in kindness and mildness. His haughty and assuming character will likewise mark him out of doors; and his pride, obstinacy, opinionativeness, touchiness, resentfulness, and violence, must have involved him in many a quarrel and brawl. He must be tremendous when drunk. He has a *prodigious* conceit of himself; and although he is not indifferent to the *praise* of others, (which, however, he seldom gets,) he snaps his fingers at their opinion when *against* him. His character is intensely selfish. There is much *savoir faire*, amounting even to cunning and hypocrisy. He is proud of being thought *deep*, studies the weak side of those with whom he deals, drives a hard and *knowing* bargain, gives truth to the winds, and glories in taking his merchant at disadvantage. He loves money, and grasps it so hard that it is difficult to get it out of his clutches for his just debts. His perceptions of justice are so feeble, that he will consider justice, if directed *against* himself, as injustice, and even injury. His money will all go for his own animal indulgences, even to the neglect of his family, when he is pinched. Charity or benevolence never drew sixpence from him. If he can both enjoy sensuality and hoard money, he will do both. He possesses very considerable intellectual powers, which will be directed steadily in the service of his propensities and selfishness. If he has failed to make money in a coarse and plentiful way, it must proceed *from his deficient Conscientiousness affecting his credit*. His intellectual manifestations are coarse and inelegant, but they have considerable vigour. He is shrewd, observing, remembering, and sagacious, with a great power of *concentrative application of mind to his purpose*. He might succeed as a draughtsman or surveyor, but does not seem to have any *mechanical genius* about him. He is probably an indifferent workman with his hands, *except in fighting*. His head is his implement. I should expect to find him unpunctual, disorderly, slovenly, and dirty. He would have figured as a warrior or *marauder* in barbarous times; *force is his engine*, and he possesses great power of character to wield it. He is not insensible to religious impressions, if they were ever pressed home upon him; but his religion will be abject and selfish, and any thing but the practical morality of Christianity.

This individual could not match shades of colour.

P. S.—On reflecting on the foregoing character, it has occurred, that although all that has been said is IN the man's nature, his *Secretiveness* and *Intellect* directing his own *interest*, may have prevented so broad a manifestation of it as to be *generally* recognised; or by any but those who have seen him long, closely, and intimately.

J. S.

AN account of the individual was subsequently drawn up by the gentleman who had sent the cast. It is as follows:—

Character of the uneducated man, deduced from a long and intimate knowledge of the individual.

I have had many opportunities of knowing well the character of this individual, which I have made a point of studying minutely, both as a matter of curiosity and as an interesting subject of philosophical speculation. He is a native of Wales, and thirty-two years of age; he stands six feet high, and is very strongly made. I am not well versed in the doctrine of the temperaments; but if there be such a temperament as the *sanguineo-melancholic*, I should say it is his. Though perfectly illiterate, and ignorant upon almost every subject, there is something about the man which makes it impossible for any body to despise him. Taken individually, all his qualifications are despicable, yet, considered in the aggregate, they are of that character which renders it difficult to view him contemptuously. His temper is decidedly bad: it is not merely quick, but obdurate and sour; and if he once conceives a dislike to any one, it is almost impossible to remove it. He is extremely jealous, pettish, and suspicious, and cannot tolerate quizzery of any description. At the same time, although on some points it is not difficult to play upon him, yet he has such an immense opinion of his own penetration, that he conceives no man could attempt such a step without being instantly detected. Any opinion which he may form he views as infallible, and all the evidence in existence will not make him abandon it. I have no doubt whatever, from what I have seen and known, that he is tyrannical and domineering. He is also very quarrelsome—so much so, that it is disagreeable to walk on the streets with him, lest he get involved in a scrape. He has no idea of accommodating himself to others, but goes doggedly along, pushing aside those who are not exactly disposed to get out of his way. He is a capital pugilist. The science of boxing he has studied indefatigably—not, as it occurs to me, as an exercise, but to render himself formidable. The consequence is, that he has got into fifty *rows;* and if, at any time, you meet him, the chances are that his eyes are either in mourning from blows received, or his knuckles injured from the punishment given to his antagonist. His habits are altogether of a low order. He has no fondness for, but rather an aversion to, elegant and virtuous female society; and his associates are mostly prize-fighters, and sporting characters generally. With regard to his amative propensity, every body acquainted with him knows that it is very great; he is, in fact, the slave of that feeling, and never speaks of a woman except in an animal point of view. I think I may safely say, that I never knew a person so perfectly indifferent to poetry, painting, fine scenery, and every thing beautiful in the material world. It is certain that the Cowgate, or Wapping, would excite about as much of the sublime in his mind as Glencoe or the Vale of Chamouni. If people in his company begin to speak of such subjects, and show any rapture, he gets gloomy and irritated, pronounces the conversation " d——d stuff," and, unless it be abandoned, he leaves the room. On the contrary, get upon fighting, and, like the war-horse, his eye instantly lightens up—he becomes the cock of the company, and describes, with intense delight, the many brawls he has been in,—shows how he pounded this man and that man, and exemplifies, in the most graphic manner imaginable, all the different details of a fight. Indeed, his stories on such subjects are master-pieces in their way. They abound in details,—are astonishingly circumstantial; and if he tells the story fifty times, it never varies. I have no doubt whatever that many of his alleged exploits are mere lies; but they are certainly the best put-together ones I ever listened to, and look prodigiously like truth. In fact, their excessive circumstantiality and detail, and the unvarying way in which he tells them, long imposed upon me, and convinced me that, in spite of their improbability, they must be true, till I ascertained from unquestionable evidence, that some of them, at least, were merely ingenious fabrications, got up for the purpose of aggrandizing himself.

He is very fond of praise, especially of his person, which he considers faultless. This, indeed, is the only vulnerable point about him, and if the thing is done judiciously, he will swallow a most enormous dose; but if he once supposes they are quizzing him, it will require no small restraint to prevent him from inflicting summary punishment on the quizzer. His great ambition is to be a first-rate boxer, or possess great strength; and so strong is the feeling, that if the choice were given him of being able to write Paradise Lost, or beat Jem Ward, there is no doubt he would fix upon the latter. Literature and literary men he views with great contempt. He says, that if he had received a proper education, and possessed the same advantages as other people, he could have written as good works as any man that ever lived. With all this he has no love whatever for reading. Indeed, he confesses,—I sincerely believe, for the purpose of making his natural genius appear more extraordinary—that he never read a volume through all his life, a fact which I perfectly credit. The only reading he ever indulges in, is the account of the prize-fights in Bell's Life in London.

One strong feature in his character is a total want of punctuality. When he makes an appointment, it is the merest chance in the world if he keeps it. Indeed, he does not seem to think there is the slightest impropriety in violating such engagements. He is also slovenly in his dress, and altogether what you would call a careless, reckless sort of being.

So far as I know the man, I should say that his character is greatly deficient in philanthropy. He is disposed to take harsh views of things, and judge people's actions uncharitably. When offended at any one, he is also prone to curse at him and abuse him without mercy. Indeed, the whole texture of his mind is singularly inelegant; and I do not believe, that, under any system of education, it would be possible to have made him, in manners or conversation, a suitable companion for well-bred people.

With regard to his conscientiousness, I really am at a loss what to say. For the first six years of my acquaintance with him, I

K

considered him the most simple-minded and honest of human beings, and, for any thing I can prove to the contrary, I might consider him so still; but I must say candidly, that some reports got into circulation against him in 1829, any thing but creditable to his honesty. He was accused (with what truth I know not) of having appropriated sums of money which did not belong to him; and a stigma was attached to his character on this account, which I sincerely hope, and almost believe, is false, but which many persons affirm to be too true. This is all I can say. Be the matter as it may, it has done him great injury, and prevented him ever since from getting respectable employment.

I have spoken of his want of punctuality. This irregular propensity is manifested in the preference he gives to dining in chop-houses to doing so in his own house, and in his fondness for late hours. Indeed, he is exceedingly unsystematic, though both shrewd, observant, and sagacious. He seems, in an argument, to be quite incapable of proceeding upon general principles; and although he will never strike his own colours, he invariably mystifies and tires out his opponents.

He is ambitious of being thought formidable in drinking and eating. I have heard him boast before ladies of the quantity of porter he could drink, and beef-steaks he could consume. He is exceedingly pleased when any one compliments him upon his amative powers; and, in short, swallows with avidity whatever tends to exalt him in the scale of manhood. The only intellectual quality which he is vain of having imputed to him is his great *penetration* and his talents for argument. He alleges, that were he better educated, he would be quite invincible at the latter accomplishment.

I think he has some mimicry about him, but it is all of the low kind. I have seen him *take off* some of his acquaintances pretty adroitly. He has also a fondness for vulgar jokes. For instance, I have seen him get hold of some half-cracked creature, and try how many pies he could eat—he himself laughing heartily, and enjoying the exhibition with great delight. I recollect of him getting a couple of fellows to try which of them would eat most rapidly a quantity of hot porridge, the winner to get five shillings for his performance. On another occasion he promised a carter two shillings if he would drink off half a gallon of small beer.

With regard to his love of money, I am at a loss what to say. Any time that I have seen him spend money, it always occurred to me as if it were done more out of a pure spirit of ostentation than from liberality. Others have frequently made the same remark. I cannot bring myself to say that any particular fondness for the acquisition of wealth on his part ever occurred

APPENDIX. 219

to me: but on this point I am not competent to speak. Of one thing, however, I am certain, that most of the money he lays out is expended in the bagnio, the chop-house, or among the pugilists. He spends little in clothing, and I believe never purchased a book in his life time.

I cannot speak of his religious feelings. I never saw any exhibited; but he has been most unfavourably situated for their manifestation. If he once took it into his head to be religious, he would be such a saint as Louis XI. or Catherine de' Medici.

In short, he is a man who may be persuaded into a thing by flattery, but it is impossible to make him move a step by any other consideration. His obstinacy is very great, and proof against almost any thing. If he were in a station where he had plenty of scope and little restraint, I think he would be extremely tyrannical and fond of inflicting punishment. I have often heard him express great rage against Colonel Brereton for not sabring the people at Bristol, and swear that if he had had the command on that occasion, he would have slaughtered them by hundreds. This I believe firmly he would not scruple to do in such circumstances. If he took a fancy for a person, and that person did exactly as he wished, I think he would sacrifice life and limb to serve him; but the slightest symptom of the individual acting independently and thinking for himself would make him cast him off. With regard to his love of children, I should think it considerable. At least children—with the exception of his three brothers to whom he is much attached—are the only people towards whom I ever observed him to take a fancy. His letters are stiff, and indicate a deficient command of language; though in his capacity of a clerk he has had plenty of experience in letter writing. His arithmetical powers are not great. I should think them below par. That he would be intensely litigious it is impossible to doubt. The expression of his face is sinister and gloomy, and indicates dogged determination and great want of mental flexibility.

REMARKS BY MR. SIMPSON ON THE PRECEDING ACCOUNT.

This character is substantially the same as that transmitted to ———. To the postscript of the latter it gives great value. In spite of six years' intimate acquaintance with, and minute study of, this singular person, Mr.——— did not know an important feature in his character—his deficient Conscientiousness, but had it only from reports. Yet he narrates several traits quite inconsistent with Conscientiousness, although he himself does not appear to observe how they bear.

No. IV.

CHANGE OF CHARACTER AND TALENTS, AND A SIMULTANEOUS CHANGE IN THE FORM OF THE HEAD.

The following observations are reprinted in the 50th number of the Phrenological Journal, from an American work, entitled "Practical Phrenology, by Silas Jones," published at Boston, in 1836.

"Great changes in moral character and talents sometimes manifest themselves in indivduals, and the question is put to the phrenologist, whether the head changes to a corresponding extent? This question requires a very candid and considerate answer.

"1. It is important to remark upon the nature of the change which takes place in character, before we attempt to account for it by a change in the size of organs.

"The first change is that which takes place before the individual arrives at maturity. During this forming period of character great changes often take place, especially in those who are about equally inclined to good and to evil practices. The different parts of character develope themselves just as circumstances draw them out at the usual age of their manifestation. More than twenty-five of the primitive faculties shew themselves during the first eighteen months, others appear at subsequent periods, and different groups claim ascendency at different times. As to all the changes of this period, there can be no question that the shape of the head will change as the character changes. However, at this period the organs change much in relative activity, without an *equally* corresponding change in size. Those organs which have never been excited by their appropriate objects will have been less active than those which have had abundant exercise; but commence the exercise of the organs by the stimulus of their own objects, and you draw them at once into activity, and, as they become active, the structure improves as well as increases in size. We must not suppose that there is no other difference in cerebral organs but that of size. The differences in *perfection of structure and tendency to activity*, arising from habits of exercise, are quite as great as those of activity. Hence, judgments formed of the strength of particular faculties, without inquiry as to the education they have received, are liable to error.

"2. Alterations which take place in the character of individuals after they arrive at maturity, are seldom any more than a change in the objects on which the faculties act. When this is the case, no change in the form of the head is to be expected. The faculty which respects talents, office, rank, and wealth, adores the Deity; and he that has turned from the worship of idols to the worship of the only true God, has brought into action no new organ; and, unless he worship with more fervour, his reverence will not be increased in activity.

"3. Changes in the form of head are only to be expected where there has been a great change in the degree of activity of organs. If organs which have been very active cease to be so, while others which have been idle are drawn into great activity, then, in a few years, we may, in many instances, be able to notice a change. This embraces the several classes of cases.

"1. Where an individual is not advanced beyond the meridian of life, and has become very thoughtful and studious for a few years, giving great exercise to the reflective organs, they will perceptibly increase in size. There are several facts which go to prove this. So, where individuals have been suddenly changed from situations which did not give much exercise and excitement to the perceptive organs, to those which required great exercise and activity of them, we may expect a sudden growth of those organs.

"But these cases are so rare, and the changes are so gradual, that much pains should be taken to collect the facts with accuracy. Mr. Deville has been engaged in taking casts of individuals at different periods and ages, for the purpose of making comparisons.

"I have several facts, founded not upon observations made from comparison of casts, but still they are such as to be entitled to our confidence. A young artist of my acquaintance had formerly been a dealer in dry goods, and, a few years since, commenced the business of portrait-painting. He had been absent for several years from his mother: when on a visit to her, she called him up to her, and, observing every part of his countenance carefully, said, ' Your forehead has altered in form since I saw you, all the lower part of it seems to be pushed out.' This was the careful observation of a fond mother, when tracing out the lineaments of a beloved son. It was no doubt true. Nearly all the perceptive organs are now very decidedly large; and he says they have increased in size since he commenced his new vocation. Young men in cities, it will be found, have greater power and activity in the perceptive organs than those who have always been in country situations. There is a constantly changing succession of objects in cities, which give ample scope and stimulus to these organs. These rapid changes are unfavourable to quiet reflection, hence the knowing organs acquire a great ascendency.

"I have noticed, in very many instances, that experienced navigators have the organs of Locality very prominent, and probably in consequence of great exercise of them. So, with blind people, these organs become very large. It is the case of a blind man in Boston, who travels in every part of that city without a guide.

"3. A third class of cases is that in which a change takes place in the feelings, as where one or two feelings become exceedingly, and almost morbidly, active for many years, as in the case of Destructiveness and Secretiveness in G. M. Gottfried. Also, in consequence of some great shock to some feeling, as to Adhesiveness, Self-Esteem, Hope, or Love of Approbation, there may be a change in the form of the head in the regions of those organs.

" I have, in hundreds of instances, seen very striking depressions in the heads of persons of mature years, but seldom in the heads of children. These depressions are most frequent at the localities of those organs which are most liable to great neglect or suffering.

" It is not to be supposed that changes in the form of the skull externally, will be co-extensive with every slight change in the habits of thought and feeling. The *organs may change greatly in activity* without such a change in volume externally as to be noticeable. The organs most used may be contiguous to others most neglected. In such a case the one would be diminished as the other increased. Neither protuberances nor depressions are to be looked for in ordinary cases. The practised phrenologist does not need them to enable him either to find the location of the organs, or the innate dispositions and talents. They are rather to be regarded as rare occurrences and curiosities, which have enabled Gall, Spurzheim, and others, to conjecture the location of organs, which have since been proved by thousands of well-observed facts, not less conclusive, although less peculiar."

This subject is more fully discussed by Dr. Andrew Combe, in the Phrenological Journal, No. 51, in which is published a remarkable case of contemporaneous change of dispositions and cerebral development, by Mr. Kirtley, surgeon at Barnard Castle.

Mr. Deville took a cast of the head of a gentleman, thirty-two years old, and a second cast when he was at the age of thirty-six. For three or four years previously to taking the first cast, this gentleman was very fond of hoarding money, and his desire of accumulating had rendered him so penurious and unhappy, that, though his property was considerable, his friends were afraid of his becoming insane from the sheer dread of being reduced to beggary. They endeavoured to reason him out of this feeling, and sent him abroad with a gentleman, by whose attention and kindness he completely overcame the propensity, and made some progress in the study of the classics and of music. Mr. Deville states, that, upon measuring and comparing the two casts, he found the head to have considerably increased in size at the situation of the organs of Benevolence, Ideality, and the Reflecting Faculties. " I have," he adds, "two well authenticated casts of a great artist, whose life is well known. The first is a mask taken in 1792, when he was about forty-five years of age; the other a cast of his head taken after death, in 1816. Now, it is well known that he became a hoarder and groveller after money during the last fifteen or twenty years of his life; nay, he became miserable from fear of coming to want, though he possessed extensive property, besides his pictures, which were of great value. Now, upon applying the callipers at Acquisitiveness, the second cast is found to be nearly four-eighths of an inch broader than that taken in 1792, while, at the same time, its height has diminished; it has become flatter at Benevolence, and wider at Acquisitiveness. To some this may appear extraordinary, and, had I known only a single instance, I should have been silent; but as I have now between fifty and sixty cases of alteration of the form of the skull, accompanied by change of character, the subject assumes an important character, and calls to the extensive investigation."

No. V.

At page 186, I have quoted an extract from a paper by Mr. Robert Cox, in the 9th volume of the Phrenological Journal. It is entitled "Observations on the Mutual Influence of the Mental Faculties," and contains some very luminous and novel views on this subject. From this interesting article I copy the following remarks :—

" Of all the causes which excite Destructiveness, the disagreeable activity of Self-Esteem is the most frequent and powerful; and, indeed, there are few occasions on which it does not partake in the suffering produced by offence of the other faculties. For, as Lord Bacon remarks, 'contempt is that which putteth an edge upon anger, as much or more than the hurt itself; and, therefore, when men are ingenious in picking out circumstances of contempt, they do kindle their anger much.' Self-Esteem, when ill-regulated, makes individuals prefer themselves to every other person, and gives them a tendency to engross as much as possible the sources of happiness for their own peculiar advantage. Such men are therefore offended when they see other people either enjoying gratifications in which they have not the good fortune to partake—the mode of activity of Self-Esteem being in this case denominated *envy*, or grasping at what they themselves are desirous to obtain, whereby the emotion of *jealousy* is produced. The occasions which give birth to envy and jealousy, vary according to the faculties which happen to be, along with Self-Esteem, energetic. Thus, an unmarried lady, possessing large organs of the domestic affections, combined with a great development of Self-esteem, will be exceedingly apt to envy such of her acquaintances as are happily married, and surrounded by a promising and healthy family; while she will harbour jealousy towards any one who endeavours to secure the affections of the man whose love she desires for herself. A self-esteeming and acquisitive individual competing for a lucrative office is jealous of his rival; and, after failing in the pursuit, regards him with envy. This pain of Self-Esteem renders him maliciously disposed towards the fortunate candidate; he bears a grudge against him, rejoices in his misfortunes, and lets slip no opportunity of blasting his reputation. In the case here supposed, there is added to envy the emotion of hatred, which is a compound of the painful emotion of Self-Esteem, or of some other faculty, with the propensity to injure or destroy.

"The weapons by which Love of Approbation is vulnerable, are slander, ridicule, and the expression of displeasure; and it is hardly necessary to say that these have a strong tendency to excite a desire to injure the person from whom they proceed. Disappointment of this feeling has a similar effect. A man who is quashed where he intends to make a splendid figure, seldom fails to bear a grudge against the person by whom he is annihilated. When both Self-Esteem and Love of Approbation are powerful—as they were in Bonaparte, for example—there is a desire not merely to be applauded and admired, but to be the grand and prominent object of applause and admiration—to walk, in short, 'the sole hero upon the stage.' Such a man is, therefore, jealous of all whom he suspects of aiming at a share of the eclat, and envies and hates them when they get more than he. Robert Burns used to be grievously offended and irritated when not made the *lion* of the company in which he was present. The noted case of David and Saul furnishes another good illustration. When the virgins, in celebrating their exploits, proclaimed that 'Saul had slain his thousands, and David his ten thousands,' the king, we are told, 'was very wroth, and the saying displeased him; and Saul eyed David from that day and forward.' An army which has been mortified and disgraced by defeat at the hands of an enemy before regarded with contempt, is apt to be extremely ferocious when at length a victory is gained. The conduct of the Duke of Cumberland's troops in the Highlands of Scotland, after the battle of Culloden, illustrates this remark. General Hawley, in particular, whose arrogance seems to have exceeded even his folly, is characterized by Mr Chambers as having been 'one of the most remorseless of all the commanding officers; apparently thinking no extent of cruelty a sufficient compensation for his loss of honour at Falkirk.'

"It is curious, and to some may appear paradoxical, that even Benevolence can act as a direct stimulus to Destructiveness. Its disagreeable excitement occurs when we witness the infliction of pain, and is called pity or compassion. The benevolent man whose Destructiveness is powerful, has, in such cases, a vivid inclination to bestow summary chastisement on the inflicter. This is well exemplified by the incident which gave occasion to the maledictory poem of Burns, written on seeing a wounded hare pass by, and in which are embodied, in nearly equal proportions, compassion for the hare, and curses on the man who had wounded it. So enraged was the poet, that he threatened to throw the sportsman into a neighbouring river. In like manner, when a crime of great atrocity is perpretated against any individual, the anger is not confined to the sufferer alone. 'There rises,' says Dr. Thomas Brown, 'in the mind of others, an emotion, not so vivid perhaps, but of the same kind, involving the same instant dislike of the injurer, and followed by the same eager desire of punishment for the atrocious offence. In periods of revolutionary tumult, when the passions of a mob, and even, in many instances, their most virtuous passions are the dreadful instruments of which the crafty avail themselves, how powerfully is this influence of indignation exemplified in the impetuosity of their vengeance ! Indignation is then truly anger. The demagogue has only to circulate some tale of oppression ; and each rushes almost instantly to the punishment of a crime, in which, though the injury had actually been committed, he had no personal interest, but which is felt by each as a crime against himself.'

"The offence which impiety, real or imagined, gives to Veneration, is not slow in calling Destructiveness into exercise." "The Crusades will readily occur to the reader as exhibiting a fearful ebullition of Destructiveness excited through the medium of Veneration."

No. VI.

The errors daily committed in speaking of genius, demonstrate strikingly the advantages possessed by the phrenological doctrine over the old philosophy. In Dr. Currie's Life of Burns I find the following passage :—

"He who has the faculties fitted to excel in poetry, has the faculties which, duly governed, and differently directed, might lead to pre-eminence in other, and, as far as respects himself, perhaps in happier, destinations. The talents necessary to the construction of an Iliad, under different discipline and application, might have led armies to victory, or kingdoms to prosperity ; might have wielded the thunder of eloquence, or discovered and enlarged the sciences that constitute the power and improve the condition of our species."

This principle is also maintained in the following passage from an article in one of the ablest of our periodicals :—

"Michael Angelo, Leonardo da Vinci, Reubens, or Titian, would have been illustrious in any line of life. Mr. Pitt or Mr. Burke, if greatness had, in Britain, been accessible by such a channel, would have made magnificent painters."—*Blackwood's Magazine,* vol. xl. p. 83.

Phrenology demonstrates the extreme fallacy of such doctrines. According to Dr. Currie's view of the case, Homer might have excelled in science, and become a Newton; but, if this reasoning is sound, it follows that Newton—who declared poetry to be ingenious nonsense—might also have become a Homer, and written a second Iliad instead of the Principia. The chief essentials to poetical excellence are imagination, and the power of embodying its productions in sublime or beautiful language; but such qualities are in no respect necessary to excel in mathematics. Again, although a man is a poet, it does not follow that he can command armies or rule kingdoms successfully, for both of these feats can be performed well without either lofty imagination or poetical language; and if he had the two latter qualities in the utmost possible degree, he would not make a better general or practical statesman than if he wanted them entirely. Demosthenes and Horace prove that distinguished orators and poets may run away panic-struck from the field of battle. Cowper occupies a high rank as a poet; but was ever man so totally destitute of warlike qualities? With respect to painting, powerful faculties of Form, Size, Constructiveness, Colouring, and Imitation, are essential to eminence in that art; but of what use are they in eloquence or statesmanship? None whatever: hence had Pitt and Burke been destitute of them, these highly-gifted men never by any possibility could have been converted into painters, while their oratory and power to guide the helm of the state would not have been in the least degree impaired by such a want. The illustrious artists mentioned in the quotation were men of surprising versatility of talent; but it cannot be doubted that in many things they would not have shone with any degree of lustre. A great painter or orator may or may not excel in other walks; but we never can infer that he does so excel merely because he chances to be great as a painter or orator. If a man eminent in one department must necessarily excel in another, why did Pope try in vain to succeed as a painter? We know that he made the attempt earnestly, and we know also that he utterly failed. Had he possessed the cerebral configuration indispensable to painting as perfectly as that which confers poetic talent, his excellence would have been equally decided in both departments. Nature, however, while she showered upon him one divine gift, denied him the other; and no more could he have rivalled the productions of any master of the pictorial art, than walked under the armour of Goliath, or wielded the club of Hercules. Cicero, in like manner, although the greatest of Roman orators, showed himself, as a poet, to be utterly ridiculous and contemptible.

APPENDIX. 227

No. VII.

The following extraordinary case of Homicidal Monomania I find published in the Athenæum. The subject of it bears a strong resemblance to the character of René Cardillac, the jeweller, as detailed in Hoffman's powerfully written tale, entitled "Mademoiselle de Scuderi:"—

"INSANE ATTACHMENT TO BOOKS.

" The Spanish papers contain the report of one of the most singular trials that for a long time has amused or interested the public. It is the trial which has recently taken place at Barcelona, of an ex-Monk, Friar Vincente, who was condemned for having committed several murders, instigated solely by his love of books. The last murder, that which led to the discovery of the assassin, was that of a poor book-vender, named Patxot, who kept his shop (a stall) under the pillars de los Encantes, at Barcelona. Friar, or ex-friar, Vincente, for he called himself Don Vincente, had, on expulsion from his convent, established himself under the same pillars, for the purpose of vending books, and had contrived to secure a good share of the literary riches of his convent on his own shelves. Like several bibliopoles amongst ourselves, Vincente, though fond of selling, was still more desirous of having and keeping; and he never parted with a genuine book-treasure without manifest reluctance. At times he was known to fly into a passion, and abuse the happy persons who purchased and were about to carry off an antique volume.

" About four months since an auction took place of the library of an old lawyer. Amongst the books was a glorious copy of the 'Furs e Ordinacions fetes per los Gloriosos Reys de Arago als Regnicols del regne de Valencia.' It was printed in 1482, by Palmart, who introduced printing into Spain. Patxot desired much to have it, but Vincente's desire was still greater. The latter bid upwards of £50 sterling, but Patxot bid still higher; and Vincente was obliged to abandon it to his rival. Patxot carried it off in triumph, but Vincente was heard to murmur vengeance. Ere a week had elapsed, the shop of Patxot was consumed by flames, and the body of the unfortunate bibliopole reduced to ashes, together, as it was supposed, with all his treasures.

" The authorities did not think of inquiring into a circumstance that seemed natural, until the number of assassinations began to attract attention. A German literateur, who visited Barcelona, had been found murdered; a curate also of the neighbourhood. This was at first attributed to political causes, until at length it was remarked that all the victims were men of studious habits. An alcalde, Don Pablo Rafael, author of many learned works, had disappeared; a judge, too, and other functionaries.

"It was forthwith rumoured that the Inquisition had been secretly re-established, and that a tribunal under its laws held mysterious sittings, and pronounced these fearful sentences, so fearfully executed. Search was made at the domiciles of all persons supposed likely to belong to such a society; and, in pursuance of this suspicion, the shop of Don, or Friar, Vincente was searched. Nothing was found but books. The Corregidor seized one of these, the 'Directorium Inquisitorum' of Gironne, as relating to his object; when the removal of the volume caused another to fall, which had been secreted behind it. This was picked up, and opened, and proved to be the 'Furs e Ordinacions,' the volume purchased so dearly at the sale by poor Patxot, and which was now found in the possession of his rival bidder. The search was continued, and another book was found, which had belonged to Don Pablo N——, another victim. Vincente was seized, confined, menaced, and at length promised to confess, upon one condition,—viz., that his collection of books should not be scattered or sold to different persons. Satisfied in this respect, Vincente made a clean breast, and repeated his confession, with full explanations respecting his conduct, on the day of his trial.

"Placed at the bar, Vincente appeared, a little, stout, dark, man, with ruddy and open countenance. Having made the sign of the cross, he thus began:—

"'I will tell the truth; I have promised it. If I have been guilty, it has been with good intentions. I wished to enrich science, and preserve its treasures. If I have done ill, punish me; but leave my books together—they have done no harm. It was most reluctantly I consented to sell my first precious book to a curate. St. John is witness I did my utmost to disgust him with it. I told him it was a bad copy, had a page in manuscript, &c.; all would not do; he paid the price, and went away. As he walked off, along the Calle Ancho, I followed him, begged him to take back his money, and return the book. He refused; and whilst I was entreating him, we reached a lone place. Wearied with his obstinacy, I took out my dagger, and stabbed him, rolled him into the ditch, and covered him with branches, and carried home my precious volume, which I see yonder on the table.'

"The President then asked if this was the only time he had killed persons for their books. Vincente replied: 'My library is too well stocked for that: no se gano Zamora en una hora—Rome was not built in a day.'

"The President bade him explain how he had dispatched the other victims. Vincente replied: 'Nothing more simple. When

I found a purchaser so obstinate as that he would have the volume, I tore out some pages, well aware that he would come back for them. When he did, I drew him into an inner room, under pretence of replacing the pages, and then dispatched him. My arm never failed me.'

" 'Did not your heart revolt at thus destroying the image of your Maker?'

" 'Men are mortal; they die sooner or later. But books are not so; they are immortal, and merit more interest.'

" 'And you committed murder merely for books?'

" 'And for what more would you? Books are the gloria de dios'—(the glory of God.)

" 'And Patxot, how did you murder him?'

" 'I got in by the window, found him asleep, threw a soaped cord about his neck, and strangled him. When he was dead I took off the cord, set fire to the bed, and withdrew.'

" The advocate of Vincente endeavoured to invalidate the evidence, by proving that the copy of the work which Patxot had bought was not unique. This he succeeded in proving; and which affected his client more than anything else,—more even than his sentence. Notwithstanding, he was condemned to the penalty of the garrote—(strangulation.")

No. VIII.

PRACTICAL DIRECTIONS FOR THE PHRENOLOGICAL EXAMINATION OF HEADS.

In the fourth edition of Mr. Combe's " System of Phrenology," vol. i. p. 110—130, ample details are given with respect to the points to be attended to, in making a prenological survey of the head. By the permission of that gentleman, I subjoin some of his remarks on this important subject; more of them, indeed, than, without such permission, I should have considered myself at liberty to extract.

" As size, *cæteris paribus*, is a measure of power, the first object ought to be to distinguish the size of the brain generally, so as to judge whether it be large enough to admit of manifestations of ordinary vigour; for, as we have already seen, if it be too small, idiocy is the invariable consequence. The second object should be to ascertain the relative proportions of the different parts, so as to determine the direction in which the power is greatest.

" It is proper to begin with observation of the more palpable differences in size, and particularly to attend to the relative proportions of the different lobes. The size of the anterior lobe is the measure of intellect. In the brain it is easily distinguished, and in the living head it is indicated by the proportion lying before Constructiveness and Benevolence. Sometimes the lower part of the frontal lobe, connected with the perceptive faculties, is the largest, and this is indicated by the space before Constructiveness extending farthest forward at the base; sometimes the upper part, connected with the reflecting powers, is the most amply developed, in which case the projection is greatest in the upper region; and sometimes both are equally developed. The student is particularly requested to resort invariably to this mode of estimating the size of the anterior lobe, as the best for avoiding mistakes. In some individuals, the forehead is tolerably perpendicular, so that, seen in front, and judging of without attending to longitudinal depth, it appears to be largely developed; whereas, when viewed in the way now pointed out, it is seen to be extremely shallow. In other words, the mass is not large, and the intellectual manifestations will be proportionately feeble.

" Besides the projection of the forehead, its vertical and lateral dimensions require to be attended to; a remark which applies to all the organs individually—each having, of course, like other objects, the three dimensions of length, breadth, and thickness.

" The posterior lobe is devoted chiefly to the animal propensities. In the brain its size is easily distinguished; and in the living head a perpendicular line may be drawn through the mastoid process, and all behind will belong to the posterior lobe. Wherever this and the basilar region are large, the animal feelings will be strong, and *vice versa*.

" The coronal region of the brain is the seat of the moral sentiments; and its size may be estimated by the extent of elevation and expansion of the head above the organs of Causality in the forehead, and of Cautiousness in the middle of the parietal bones. When the whole region of the brain rising above these organs is shallow and narrow, the moral feelings will be weakly manifested; when high and expanded, they will be vigorously displayed.

" After becoming familiar with the general size and configuration of heads, the student may proceed to the *observation of individual organs;* and, in studying them, the real dimensions, including length, breadth, and thickness, and not the mere prominence of each organ, should be looked for.

" The length of an organ, including its supposed apparatus of communication, is ascertained by the distance from the *medulla oblongata* to the peripheral surface. A line passing through the head from one ear to the other, would nearly touch the *medulla oblongata,* and hence the external opening of the ear is assumed as a convenient point from which to estimate length. The breadth of an organ is judged of by its peripheral expansion; for it is a general law of physiology, that the breadth of an organ throughout its whole course bears a relation to its expansion at the surface: the optic and olfactory nerves are examples in point.

"The *whole* organs in a head should be examined, and their relative proportions noted. Errors may be committed at first; but without practice, there will be no expertness. Practice, with at least an average endowment of the organs of Form, Size, Individuality, and Locality, are necessary to qualify a person to make observations with success. Individuals whose heads are narrow between the eyes, and little developed at the top of the nose, where these organs are placed, experience great difficulty in distinguishing the situations and minute shades in the proportions of different organs. If one organ be much developed, and the neighbouring organs very little, the developed organ will present an elevation or protuberance; but if the neighbouring organs be developed in proportion, no protuberance can be perceived, and the surface is smooth. The student should learn from books, plates, and casts, or personal instruction (and the last is by far the best,) to distinguish the *form* of each organ, and its *appearance* when developed in different proportions to the others, because there are slight modifications in the position of them in each head.

"The prenological bust shows the situations of the organs, and their proportions, only in one head; and it is impossible by it to communicate more information. The different appearances in all the varieties of relative size, must be discovered by inspecting a *number* of heads; and especially by contrasting instances of extreme development with others of extreme deficiency. No adequate idea of the foundation of the science can be formed until this is done. In cases of extreme size of single organs, a close approximation to the *form* delineated on the bust, (leaving angles out of view) is distinctly perceived.

"The question will perhaps occur—If the relative proportions of the organs differ in each individual, and if the phrenological bust represents only their *most common proportions*, how are their boundaries to be distinguished in any particular living head? The answer is, By their *forms* and *appearances*. Each organ has a form, appearance, and situation, which it is possible, by practice, to distinguish in the living head, otherwise Phrenology cannot have any foundation.

"When one organ is very largely developed, it encroaches on the space usually occupied by the neighbouring organs, the situations of which are thereby slightly altered. When this occurs, it may be distinguished by the greatest prominence being near the centre of the large organ, and the swelling extending over a portion only of the other. In these cases the *shape* should be attended to; for the form of the organ is then easily recognised, and is a sure indication of the particular one which is largely developed. The observer should learn, by inspecting a skull, to distinguish the mastoid process behind the ear, as also bony excrescences sometimes formed by the sutures, and several bony prominences which occur in every head, from elevations produced by development of brain.

" In observing the *appearance* of individual organs, it is proper to begin with the largest, and select extreme cases. The mask of Mr. Joseph Hume may be contrasted with that of Dr. Chalmers for Ideality; the organ being much larger in the latter than in the former. The casts of the skulls of Burns and Haggart may be compared at the same part; the difference being equally conspicuous. The cast of the Reverend Mr. M. may be contrasted with that of Dempsey, in the region of Love of Approbation; the former having this organ large, and the latter small. Self-Esteem in the latter, being exceedingly large, may be compared with the same organ in the skull of Dr. Hette, in whom Love of Approbation is much larger than Self-Esteem. Destructiveness in Bellingham may be compared with the same organ in the skulls of the Hindoos; the latter people being in general tender of life. Firmness large, and Conscientiousness deficient, in King Robert Bruce, may be compared with the same organs reversed in the cast of the head of a lady (Mrs. H.) which is sold as illustrative of these organs. The object of making these contrasts is to obtain an idea of the different *appearances* presented by organs, when very large and very small.

" The terms used by the Edinburgh phrenologists to denote the gradations of size in the different organs, in an increasing ratio, are

Very small	Moderate	Rather large
Small	Rather full	Large
Rather small	Full	Very large.

" Sir John Ross has suggested, that numerals may be applied with advantage to the notation of development. He uses decimals; but these appear unnecessarily minute. The end in view may be attained by such a scale as is given in Appendix No. I.

" With respect to the practical employment of the scale above described, it is proper to remark, that as each phrenologist attaches to the terms small, moderate, full, &c. shades of meaning perfectly known only to himself and those accustomed to observe heads along with him, the separate statements of the development of a particular head by two phrenologists, are not likely to correspond entirely with each other. It ought to be kept in mind, also, that these terms indicate only the relative proportions of the organs to each other in the same head; but as the different organs may bear the same proportions in a small and in a large head, the terms mentioned do not enable the reader to discover whether the head treated of be, in its general magnitude, small, moderate, or large. To supply this information, measurement by callipers is resorted to;

but this is used not to indicate the dimensions of particular organs, for which purpose they are not adapted, but merely to indicate the *general size* of the head.

" It ought to be kept constantly in view, in the practical application of Phrenology, that it is the size of each organ in proportion to the others *in the head of the individual observed*, and not their *absolute size*, or their size in reference to any standard head, that determines the predominance in him of particular talents or dispositions."

NEW EDITIONS OF WORKS,

BY GEORGE COMBE.

A SYSTEM OF PHRENOLOGY,

Fourth Edition,

With numerous Cuts and Coloured Illustrations of the Temperaments, 2 vols. 8vo. pp. 933. Price 21s.

ELEMENTS OF PHRENOLOGY.

Fourth Edition,

With numerous Cuts and Lithographic Engravings, 12mo., pp. 194. Price 3s. 6s.

THE CONSTITUTION OF MAN,

CONSIDERED IN RELATION TO EXTERNAL OBJECTS.

Seventh Edition,

12mo, pp. 382. Price 4s.; and

THE PEOPLE'S EDITION, royal 8vo, pp. 110. Price 1s. 6d.

In consequence of the increasing demand for this Work, the present impressions extend to 10,000 Copies of The People's Edition, and 3000 Copies of the 12mo. Edition.

OUTLINES OF PHRENOLOGY.

Sixth Edition, 8vo. Price 1s.

LECTURES ON POPULAR EDUCATION.

Second Edition, 12mo. Price 2s. boards.

Just Published,

THE PHRENOLOGICAL JOURNAL,

No. 50, December, 1836.

SELECTIONS FROM THE PHRENOLOGICAL JOURNAL.

Edited by ROBERT COX.

12mo., pp. 360.   Price 5s. 6d.

LONGMAN & CO. AND SIMPKIN, MARSHALL, & CO. LONDON.
MACLACHLAN & STEWART, EDINBURGH.

Lately Published,

BY JOHN SYMINGTON & CO.

81, Queen-Street, Glasgow:

And sold by OLIVER AND BOYD:—EDINBURGH.
AND WHITTAKER & CO.—LONDON.

Neatly Printed in 18mo, *bound in Cloth, Price* 2s. 2nd Edition

DR. BRIGHAM'S CELEBRATED WORK

ON THE INFLUENCE OF

MENTAL CULTIVATION UPON HEALTH.

With an Introduction and additional Notes and Illustrations,

BY DR. MACNISH.

" Many of my readers will be glad to learn that Dr. Brigham's little work has been lately reprinted in this country in a very cheap form, under the care of Dr. Macnish of Glasgow, who is already well known as an able and successful writer, and who has enriched his edition with a number of excellent notes."—*Dr. Combe's Physiology, Fourth Edition.*

" Dr. Macnish has considerably augmented its value by the numerous notes which he has added. Besides happily illustrating many of Dr. Brigham's arguments, he has corrected one or two inaccuracies into which that intelligent physician had been led."
—*Phrenological Journal.*

Printed in Great Britain
by Amazon